To the customers of
Poulton Post Office Stores without
whom neither the shop
nor this book
would exist

CONTENTS

Title	Page
Introduction	7
The Start of it All	9
Innocents Abroad	23
Talking Shop	45
Mid-Term Blues	101
Wider Issues	151
Last Orders	197

Also by Stuart Russell: *Unjust Deserts*. A novel

OLD JOKE

One evening, a village shopkeeper, having closed his shop and completed his chores, sat disconsolately at his kitchen table. The previous day his only son had emigrated to America and he was afraid it would be years before he saw him again.

As he poured himself a whisky there was a knock at the door. "Probably somebody who's forgotten to buy something at the supermarket," he thought as he went to see who it was. But the man who stood there wasn't a customer - or if he was, he was the strangest customer the shopkeeper had ever seen.

"Mr. O' Store?"

The shopkeeper nodded.

"You don't know me," the stranger said, "but I'm here to tell you that you have won first prize in the Independent Grocer competition." Mr. O' Store had forgotten all about the competition. It had been months ago and he never had much luck in competitions anyway. "And," the man continued. "I am your prize."

The shopkeeper was a little taken aback and the man quickly reassured him. "Not me personally, you understand, but what I can do. I am a magician." He gave an extravagant bow. "And I am here to grant you a wish."

The shopkeeper blinked. "What, any wish?"

The magician bowed again. "Any wish. As one of my famous predecessors is reputed to have said, "Your wish is my command". So tell me what you would like most in the world and I will do my best to provide it."

The shopkeeper's face lit up.

"I know what I want. My son has gone to live in America and I'm afraid I shall never see him again because I get seasick when I sail and I'm terrified of flying. Now, you said any wish?"

"I did."

The shopkeeper took a deep breath. "What I would really like you to do is build me a bridge across the Atlantic."

The magician blinked. "A bridge?"

The shopkeeper nodded. "A suspension bridge."

"Across the Atlantic?"

The shopkeeper nodded again and the magician took a deep breath. "You realise how far it is across the Atlantic. Three thousand miles. You want me to build a suspension bridge three thousand miles long?"

"If you can."

The magician shook his head. "No, I'm sorry it's impossible. To be frank, it's an outrageous wish. It would use up all my magic and I'm not sure I could do it anyway. I'm sorry, but you'll have to give me another wish."

For a moment the shopkeeper looked disappointed but then again his face brightened.

"I do have another wish. As you see, I'm a village shopkeeper. And, as you probably know, these are hard times for village shops. What I would like is for you to get the people in the village to support my shop and make sure it survives."

"What, get people to support a village shop?"

"Yes."

"All the people in the village?"

The shopkeeper nodded. "Give or take…"

The magician stood up and paced around. He scratched his head, he furrowed his brow. Eventually he turned to the shopkeeper.

"This suspension bridge," he said, "How many lanes would you like?"

PART ONE

THE START OF IT ALL

PROLOGUE

In the early months of 1997, Lizzie and I came to a decision. Tired of the ongoing battle against officialdom and retailing trends, we decided to leave Poulton Post Office Stores. We'd been there for twelve years, established a base in a beautiful part of the country and provided security for our children. We had exploited the potential of the property by converting our barn into a three-bedroomed cottage, and we had almost trebled the profit from the business. So after weighing up the financial pros and cons, we decided to sell up.

We had no idea what the response would be when we put the business on the market but were determined to ensure that the shop stayed open. Selling the property as a private house could have been more lucrative but we remembered the advice we had been given twelve years before: "The shop belongs to the village. It was there before you came and as long as the villagers give you a reasonable living from managing it, it's your duty to see that it's there after you leave." Well the villagers - or a substantial minority of them - *had* given us a reasonable living so we felt honour bound to keep the shop open. Not only that, we planned to stay in Poulton and didn't want to live in a village without a shop. We obtained several valuations but before we'd settled on an agent, friends from a neighbouring village invited us to supper.

Before we went I'd had a dream that Rob, our host, was wearing one of my suits and although he is a good deal shorter than I am, it fitted him perfectly. When we told them about the dream, Rob's wife Sue looked astonished and asked whether the suit had "subpostmaster" on the lapel. We were mystified but later in the evening both her comment and her astonishment became clear.

Rob and Sue were thinking of buying our shop and saw the dream as a significant omen. On such "evidence" are choices made and lives changed.

But we were astonished. We couldn't believe that Rob and Sue would want to give up their idyllic country cottage to run a village post office. Rob was a video editor, a job he assured us was far less interesting and glamorous than it sounded. We tried to put them off, emphasised all the pitfalls, didn't want recriminations if they went through with it and the venture failed. But their hearts were set on it and as G.K. Chesterton remarked there is a road from the eye to the heart which doesn't go through the intellect. In fairness, Rob also presented sound reasons for his decision - the insecurity of film editing, the stressful trips to London, the fifteen-hour days – and he finally convinced us he was serious, that he would change neither his mind nor his heart.

So the deal was struck and Rob and Sue are now installed in Poulton Post Office and Lizzie and I are enjoying a life of such leisure that we have found time to write a book about our experiences as village shopkeepers.

Village shops. The words conjure up a calmer, more considerate world where the pace was slower and the service element stronger. Their demise has coincided with the transformation of this older safer world into a world of superstores, where communities are breaking down, and where the remaining village shopkeepers struggle to compete with increased competition, increased bureaucracy and indifference from local residents. This was the world we entered in the spring of 1986 when we took over Poulton Post Office and began to experience the mixed blessings of running a village stores and were introduced to the intricacies and intimacies of life in a small village. We tried to run the shop with a mixture of efficiency and humour believing that, above all, customers had to enjoy their visits and want to return. It seems we succeeded as in 1996, on the strength of a flood of commendations, we won the Gloucestershire Village Shop of the Year award. At a time when many similar establishments were on their last legs, we achieved an eighty per cent increase in profits above the rate of inflation and transformed the shop from a moderate business sailing close to the economic wind into a successful enterprise that we could hand on with confidence. Our years running the shop were full of humour and pathos, excitement and sadness, satisfaction and frustration. Above all it was a time of regular contact with people and all their fascinating foibles because in a village shop, as a certain Sunday newspaper used to claim, "all human life is there".

CHAPTER ONE

A CHANGE OF DIRECTION

"You're thinking of what? I asked as a friend and I chewed over job prospects at the end of our careers in African education.

"Buying a post office."

"Are you mad? You know nothing about post offices."

"I do."

"What?"

"They sell stamps. Anyway it's just an idea."

"A pretty crazy idea if you ask me."

"At least I've *got* an idea. You haven't a clue what you're going to do."

"Yes I have. I've applied for a job with the British Council in Khartoum. *And* I'm writing a romantic novel."

He gave a snort . "A romantic novel! And you say I'm mad."

"Mills and Boon pay £20,000 a book. How much do post offices pay?"

"Not that much but at least it's guaranteed. A romantic novel? Now I've heard it all."

He was still muttering as we went our separate ways. A few years later he was churning out bodice rippers by the sackful. And making a fortune.

As for me…I bought a post office.

The decision was partly dictated by economic logic. I had returned to England after fifteen years to find that cuts in the education budget had made a career in teaching extremely problematic. On the wrong side of forty, I was in limbo and wanted a more secure existence than contractual employment in the Third World. (More secure? A village post office? I can hear the cries of disbelief as I write). I did go to Khartoum but it wasn't a long-term solution. A three-year contract and then what? Another scratching around for bits of work, for some kind of income? No thanks. Lizzie and I needed something more stable, more secure. And we opted for a post office.

" MILLS AND BOON PAY £20,000 . . . . . "

I really did think my friend had taken leave of his senses when he talked about buying a post office but the more we thought about it the more attractive it became. We had set three conditions for future employment: stability, a regular income, and a job we could do as a partnership. Buying a post office satisfied all of them.

I think we also saw it as a soft option, something that any intelligent person could do. I'm sure this is why many people looking for a change of direction consider buying post offices. No expertise or qualifications needed, minimal re-training, just save a deposit and buy a nice home with an income attached.

Surprisingly it was almost that simple.

We started our search in the spring of 1985 when I made a forty-eight-hour trip from Khartoum to look at a place in the Home Counties. It wasn't suitable. Next we viewed a lock up run by a workaholic called Dale, an "open-all-hours" establishment which didn't conform to our idea of the good life at all. Mr Dale wasn't even sure what kind of house he lived in, he was at home so rarely. The next place we looked at was also run by people called Dale and we began to wonder whether having the name "Dale" wasn't a pre-requisite for running a post office.

This was the start of a summer of disappointments. At the out-set, we had imagined hundreds of suitable businesses just begging to be taken over by two young(ish), intelligent, enthusiastic people but after drawing repeated blanks we began to feel like the blind man looking for the black hat in the dark cellar as we ran the rule over some dreadful businesses that on paper sounded quite prom-ising. We learned to take the agents' descriptions with a large pinch of salt: "small, well-kept garden" (little more than a window box), " vast potential" (the house or the business - probably both - in an appalling state), "neat and compact property" (no room to swing a cat), and so on. The worst example was when a "coach house" turned out to be a garden shed.

" A SMALL, EASILY MANAGED GARDEN...."

Eventually, prepared for another disappointment, we jour-neyed to the Cotswolds to look at the post office in the little village of Filkins. In fact, Filkins post office turned out to be the first real possibility. The house was nice - no better than nice but substan-tially better than anything else we'd seen - and the business, though not exactly thriving, wasn't bad enough to put us off. So in spite of several doubts, we went ahead and made an offer.

But oh those doubts! The village had recently been by-passed so passing trade was non-existent. Also there were other people interested and the vendor, a betting man, was running a first-past-the-post system - the first person to come up with the money would clinch the deal – by which time the unsuccessful applicants would be deep into debt and probably homeless. Then during one of our visits, we chatted to a woman from the nearby council estate who described the place as "a dying shop in a dying village" and we drove away despondent. Did we really want to commit our future to a dying shop in a dying village? It wasn't a happy prospect and only a kind of fatalism drove us on. We were deeply involved and short of options, and would only withdraw in the unlikely event of something better turning up.

" ... in a much sought-after location"

In September, the day before I returned to Khartoum for my final stint, we received details of a post office in another Cotswold village. The salary and turnover were comparable to Filkins but the property sounded much more interesting. We arranged to view the place on the way to Heathrow but by the working of the infernal law attributed to Sod, the car broke down and it was eleven o'clock the next morning before we could hire a replacement. It was now too late to visit the new post office *and* catch my flight so Lizzie dropped me at Heathrow and visited the place alone.

So as I was sitting on a Balkan Airways flight, sipping Bulgarian champagne and being tended to by stern-faced hostesses, Lizzie was introducing herself to the cynical Brummie who preceded us at Poulton, and making the decision that would shape the rest of our lives, the decision to buy Poulton Post Office. We abandoned Filkins with relief, writing it off as part of the learning process. It had at least given us a yardstick and Lizzie was able to make an offer for Poulton without consulting me as, incredibly, it was on offer at the same price. Filkins had passed its peak and offered little in the way of potential, while Poulton was a property and business bursting with possibilities. The only concern was that there was another shop in the village but Lizzie was assured that the owners were near retirement age and would close the shop within two years. As a footnote, Filkins Post Office closed within two years as well and if we'd taken it over - and assuming that even *our* personalities and dynamism couldn't have reversed the tide of the inevitable! - our little project would have died in its infancy.

The sale was agreed within days and after a few hiccups the cynical Brummie and his wife (otherwise known as Harold and Jessie) couldn't have been more helpful. Mind you, the hiccups lasted several months. My commitments in Khartoum didn't end until December but I managed a week's leave before then and made my first visit to the village that was to become our home.

The house was a traditional four-bedroomed property with a convertible loft, an impressive array of outbuildings and a far larger garden than any we'd seen on our previous forays into the post office market. There was a walled garden outside the oak-beamed sitting room and as we walked round it, a fox emerged from the undergrowth, bounded up the lean-to roof and disappeared over the adjoining barn. Our impression of the idyllic rural retreat was complete.

I returned to Khartoum and the serious phase of the sale began. Harold was on the phone constantly, talking non-stop and making uncomplimentary remarks about our solicitor simply because the poor man was insisting on certain formalities to protect our interests. "What do you think of that then?" he barked after one monologue lasting several minutes. "Speechless, eh! Just like me!" On one document he was listed as Garold which rather summed him up.

But his impatience was understandable in the light of what we learned later. This was the second time the property had been on the market and a deal agreed. The first "buyers" were having a cup of tea and a walk in the garden when the woman noticed the loft window. It was shrouded in cobwebs and when she asked about it, Jessie replied: "That's where the Post Office ghost lives."

The response was cataclysmic. The next day Harold received a call from the British Society for Psychic Research who had been asked by the woman to investigate the property. Harold's scepticism on such matters makes Doubting Thomas seem like an unquestioning believer and one can imagine his feelings as the researchers tapped away at floors and walls, exchanging telling glances and making copious notes. They must have found something as a few days later the purchase offer was withdrawn and, instead of retiring to their bungalow in the Malvern Hills, Harold and Jessie found themselves back in the post office and the business back on the market. When I first phoned Harold expressing interest and in the next breath informed him that I was leaving the country, his thoughts were probably unprintable. First he loses a sale because the buyers think the place is haunted, then he has a phone call from a bloke on the point of emigrating! He could have been forgiven for thinking that all people interested in Poulton Post Office were a few dockets short of a pension book. But the sale went ahead and we can only be grateful to the ghost for making it possible. We had a few "close encounters" ourselves and always found the ghost a benign presence.

Once contracts had been exchanged and a completion date set, Harold gave us as much help as he could. During our first week, while I was receiving my post office training, Jessie helped to run the shop and Harold took Lizzie through one complete cycle of stock ordering. They led us gently through the shallows and it wasn't until they left, on the second Saturday, that we suffered our first attack of stage fright. By then we'd begun the process of settling into our new life and conditioning ourselves to the fact that we were now officially classed as shopkeepers.

I cast my mind back to the shops of my childhood, dark little places with dirty wooden counters and a strange assortment of dusty products. Some of them were called sweet shops though there was nothing sweet about the women who shuffled to the counter from the living quarters at the back. Shopkeepers evoked memories of a less sophisticated age, before Environmental Health Officers and sell-by dates, before electronic tills and computers. No new business ideas threatened their mindsets and the word "market" would have meant nothing except the place with stalls in the town centre.

Was this then the culmination of our romantic dreams, becoming part of this class disparagingly referred to as "shopkeepers"? Graduates with minds broadened by a range of travel and an even greater range of interests, did we really want to become part of this retailing subculture where people sold their souls for a couple of quid and would cut their grannies' throats rather than cut prices?

We answered in an uncertain affirmative. We would upgrade the image of shopkeepers, reveal them as people who listened to classical music, went to art galleries, watched wildlife and travel programmes, preferred Jeremy Paxman to Bruce Forsyth, asked for a good claret instead of a sweet sherry and didn't see Indian food as synonymous with Vesta. After all, we told ourselves, if *we* wanted to be shopkeepers, then shopkeepers couldn't be as uncouth as people thought.

Either that, or we weren't as sophisticated as we liked to believe.

CHAPTER TWO

BURNING OUR BOATS

"On the first of May, It is moving day," I crooned, mimicking a Mel Torme hit of the fifties. Our moving day didn't have quite the same undertones. It was early March, not May, and we were moving into a new life and a job that we neither had experience of nor understood. In a flush of enthusiasm - which Lizzie didn't entirely share - I had suggested we hired a van and moved ourselves. "G.K. Chesterton says that a nuisance is an adventure looked at in a different way," I assured her. It didn't cut much ice.

The sale hadn't proceeded without a few hitches at our end of the chain. Our buyers, having no experience of the tortuous procedures involved in anything to do with the Post Office, had expected everything to be signed and delivered within a few weeks. When it wasn't, they turned nasty and said that unless we contributed towards their hotel bills and storage charges, the deal was off. I phoned Harold who, never reluctant to call a spade a shovel, fumed, "There's a word for this. Blackmail." He was right but rather than risk the whole selling edifice crumbling, he agreed to go halves.

Moving day arrived to find us half-packed and half-prepared (half-baked is another description). The kids went off to school and we didn't expect to see them again until the following Monday as our neighbour, Karen, was picking them up from the bus and taking them to stay with friends for the weekend. Our buyers had planned to move in some time after midday and we assured them this wouldn't be a problem. I collected the van from Leicester and we started loading

We worked until lunch by which time the house was less than half empty even though the van was more than half full. When I'd told the hire company that we were moving the contents of a two-and-a-half bedroomed cottage, they had recommended a Luton van. I looked at the Luton and had serious doubts. "Even people in semis don't need anything bigger than a Luton," I was told, "but if you're worried, take the next size up. Then you'll be absolutely certain."

After a quick lunch, we resumed our task. The van was filling up at a rate of knots but we were making little impression on the flood of furniture pouring from the house. It astonished us that we possessed so much and although we suspected that a lot of it was rubbish, we hadn't the heart - or the time - to discriminate. In it all went and the illusion of space was vanishing with the day.

The purchasers' van arrived around two o'clock, precise and orderly, and the removal men began unloading. Our stuff was going out of the back door as theirs was coming in the front. I had visions of most of it coming straight through the house and into our van - except there wouldn't be room. The children came back (where had the day gone?) to find furniture piled on the tailgate, suitcases in the gutter, washing machine and tumble drier blocking the rear entrance. Karen whisked them away (the children that is).

We were four hours behind schedule and furniture was still pouring into the street. It had long become clear that even this "oversize" van wouldn't take all our goods and chattels and we explained to the buyers that we would have to leave the overflow in the outhouse overnight. Relations which had been strained before, now threatened to boil over, particularly as they had been under the mistaken impression that we were leaving our cooker and hadn't expected to find a gaping hole in the kitchen.

By the time we left, Mel Torme and G.K. Chesterton had long given way to Laurel and Hardy. The van was bulging at the sides and I had visions of the contents cascading out when we opened it in Poulton. But at least we were on our way, leaving the old life behind like the pioneers of old. And as we set off - literally "into the sunset" - it seemed as if the "nuisance" bit might at last be behind us and the "adventure" part about to begin.

But reality soon pushed romance into the background. The van was due back in Leicester at seven the following morning and we tried not to think of all the things we had to do before then. It was almost nine by the time we reached Poulton and well after ten by the time our belongings were unloaded and stored in the little barn next to the main house. Harold insisted on helping, more we suspected out of a misguided machismo than anything else and the sight of him carrying a chest of drawers the wrong way with the whole length protruding from his body like a huge rectangular beer gut is a memory we treasure to this day, particularly as Jessie had warned him to "watch your heart."

A friend who was holidaying in Africa had offered us the use of her bungalow near Oxford where we planned to squeeze in a few hours sleep. We left Poulton about half past ten and picked up a Chinese meal from a nearby town, a ritual repeated on many a Friday night when we had finished the post office balance. But that night the balance and everything else to do with the Post Office were a long way ahead. It was after midnight when we reached the bungalow and as we put on the gas fire and heated up the take away, we felt the tension leave us. Tired and hungry, we could have stayed in that little haven of warmth and comfort forever.

Forever turned out to be about five hours and before the sun was up we were back on the road to Leicester where we exchanged the van for a smaller model to take the rest of our belongings. We stumbled into a rattly blue Bedford and set off for breakfast with the people we now sadly had to think of as our *ex*-neighbours.

If the bungalow in Oxford had provided us with order and comfort, Karen's house that morning provided it in spades. Amid worrying thoughts that our lives were in a state of flux with some of our belongings in our old house next door, others in the out-buildings at Poulton, the children somewhere else and all for a venture which was at best uncertain, you can imagine what it was like to encounter something recognisably normal. I had reluctantly come round to Lizzie's view; a nuisance is nothing like an adventure, whatever name you give it. We made two further trips to Poulton, one in the Bedford, the other in our car, each vehicle full to the brim. Then it was up to Nottinghamshire for a week with Lizzie's parents before setting off finally to Poulton and the real beginning of our adventure.

Or perhaps the start of an unbelievable nuisance.

PART TWO

INNOCENTS ABROAD

CHAPTER ONE

IN AT THE DEEP END

So we became shopkeepers in a little village of around three hundred people where the bizarre rubs shoulders with the commonplace. Recent residents of Poulton have included a self-styled witch, a psychiatrist, two unrelated people who took part in a round-the-world yacht race, a couple who ran a restaurant in Hollywood, a translator of grand opera, a presenter of the television programme *Tomorrow's World*, a man who bought a helicopter to thwart a drink-driving ban, a heroine of the French Resistance, a clairvoyant, an auctioneer, a World War Two pilot, a woman who filled her house with dogs, a victim of the Lloyds' crash, a colonic irrigationist, the brother and sister of two acclaimed travel writers, a BBC journalist, a couple whose retirement romance featured in a woman's magazine, a nationally acclaimed mountain bike business, at least one crook, a man who spent two years on the run, the great grand-daughter of Charles Dickens, the great niece of Clem Attlee......the list goes on. Gentleman farmers, captains of industry, retired army officers, financiers, computer experts, a racing tipster, an American eccentric, all mingle with pensioners, farm workers, teachers. And the place they mingle is the village shop.

I was recently looking at a book called *The Gloucestershire Village Book* compiled by the Gloucestershire Federation of Women's Institutes. The following is an extract about Poulton:

"Before 1940 there was a school, two public houses - the New Inn, (an ale house) and the Falcon, fully licensed. In addition we had a post office with a manual telephone exchange combined with a cycle shop and a saddler; three grocery shops - one with a bakery attached; one with a butcher attached; one selling papers. There was also a separate baker.... and a blacksmith at the Old Forge.... Milk was brought round to the door in cans and measured into one's jug..."

What a lively community Poulton must have been in those days. Now it's been reduced to just one shop, which doubles up as a post office - and one pub. John Major's vision of rural England - old ladies cycling to church, warm ale, the sound of leather on willow - relates more to the era described in the Gloucestershire Village book than to the present. In those days the population would have been totally dependent on farming - landowners, tenant farmers, labourers plus the shops and professions that supported them. Now a great deal has changed. Much has been gained in the process but something vital has been lost. Including, in Poulton, five or six shops.

This was the world we committed ourselves to in 1986; the village of Poulton, and the responsibility of running one of the institutions that gave the village its identity. And committed is precisely what we were, certainly for the first two years. We had to get to know the customers for a start, this melange of the mad and the mundane, and convince them that the new people in their shop were user-friendly. We had to find out who the regulars were, who we could rely on for sustained custom, who lived in Poulton and who came from outside, who already had accounts and who else should be allowed credit. Harold had covered a lot of this but there is a limit to how much can be digested in a short time. We also had to learn patience and tolerance – with the customer who spent half the morning buying two rashers of bacon, with the old woman who stank the place out, with the battle axe who threatened to wrap tins of sardines round my head, with the couple who tried every trick in the book to increase their weekly credit, and with many many more.

Then there was the home delivery service to cope with. Every Friday Harold would deliver orders to several customers in and around Poulton. He took me on the round a couple of times but there were still a few occasions when I mixed up the boxes and a teetotaller would find two bottles of sherry in her order. The reactions to such mistakes - amusement or irritation - told us a lot about the people concerned.

There was also the ordering of stock. We were fortunate at the start to be serviced by Londis which meant that one of our major fears - regular trips to the cash and carry - didn't materialise until several years later. Londis was a godsend but there were many items they didn't deliver - bread, frozen food, biscuits, fresh pork, wine, vegetables, cards, tights, batteries, shoe laces, meat pies - wherever we looked there was stock to order, shelves to fill, prices to decide, profit margins to determine.

Not to mention the post office. Even "easy" things like postage were far from straightforward. Take overseas mail, a few dozen postage rates to a hundred different destinations, each of which was classified as Zone 1, 2 or 3. Some had customs labels, some didn't. There was swiftair, small packages, printed paper, overseas parcels (economy) and overseas parcels (standard) each with different prices, labels and documentation. And each country had different restrictions - on sizes, weights, and what could be sent by post. Inland, there was registered mail, special delivery, recorded mail, compensation fee parcels, advice of delivery, certificates of posting - we're still on postage, remember! Then there were the different benefit books for pensions, income support, child benefit, disability allowance etc, and the stop orders, green giros, giro inpayments with standard fee payable, giro inpayments with no fee payable, giro outpayments, business cash deposits, cheque deposits, cashing other banks cheques, postal orders of different denominations and with five different levels of stamp duty, motor vehicle licences with several taxation classes and prices and different forms for customers who had received their notifications from DVLA than for those who hadn't. There were savings bank inpayments and outpayments, warrants, saving certificates, premium bonds, TV Licences (colour and black and white) telephone bills, electricity bills, water rates, council rates, local authority rents, fishing licences, game licences, even at the beginning, dog licences. Each of these transactions had different accounting procedures with different forms and different envelopes. Some were sent daily, some weekly. And every Friday night, the postmaster's ultimate horror...

THE BALANCE!!

.....when all the transactions of the week had to be totalled and balanced against stock and cash in hand.....and you prayed the two figures would be reasonably close. Otherwise, out you went on your Friday night jaunt (well, occasionally) trying to lose yourself in a play, a film or just a few beers with a £250 deficit hanging over your head.

At the start, the balance was a mystery, a weekly meandering through a bureaucratic maze strewn with all the hazards of a week's transactions. After a while it became clearer. We understood the route and the possible hazards - inverting the figures, adding things up wrong, miscounting, leaving a docket in a pension book, counting a cheque inpayment as a cash inpayment, putting a Premium Bond prize on the wrong side of the National Savings return, taking last week's deficit off when it should have been added on (weird, isn't it?). But clarifying the problems made little difference to our ability to reach a satisfactory conclusion. Knowing *how* to do the balance didn't mean we could actually *do* the balance, (like knowing how to swim the Channel or how to climb Everest). Even after twelve years we were still (occasionally) getting deficits or surpluses of over £100 but by then we realised it didn't matter very much. Or were we just past caring?

How postmasters cope with the balance depends on how readily they tolerate mistakes. Mrs Brown, the postmistress in our previous village, would reputedly stay up half the night looking for 4p. 40p would bring on the black shakes. Harold told us not to take things this seriously. "The Post Office won't worry if it's £4 out either way so why should you?" We increased this - not entirely through choice - to £40 either way. During his second or third month Rob leapt into a different financial universe - £400 as an acceptable imbalance - either way. What would Mrs Brown make of it all, one wonders?

Even apart from the balance, the post office was still bewildering. On the top shelf was a collection of black folders - *The Post Office Guide*, *A Guide to Counters Transactions*, *Motor Vehicle Licensing*, etc. – each presumably a fount of vital information. At the start I used to cast guilty glances towards the top shelf as another week went by and I still hadn't found the time - or the inclination - to begin what I thought was my essential reading. It was a bit like I'd felt at university when I thought of how few nineteenth century novels I'd read for someone considered an expert on the nineteenth century novel. These black files were the reference section of our little post office. They reminded me of the library in Khartoum Polytechnic where some books had never left the shelves. A book on plant ecology had been taken out once - on 18th October 1963. Twelve copies of *My Life as the First Lady* by Ladybird Johnson had an incongruous permanence about them and not one to my knowledge had ever been opened. Their only purpose seemed to fill a space. The black folders on our top shelf were there for a similar reason – to give some point to the shelving.

But there were so many of them, a bureaucratic *War and Peace*, an *Encyclopaedia Bureaucratica* in ten volumes. We did our job - somehow - and apart from an occasional - and usually abortive - attempt to solve a counters problem, the folders remained in place, as much a mystery at the end as at the beginning.

The Post Office also provided us with a "Magazine Section" consisting of *The Courier*, *The Subpostmaster*, and *Counters Bulletin* - as well as special notices bizarrely called *Emergency Cascades*. There was also *Brief Encounter* - though not the kind experienced by Trevor Howard and Celia Johnson with Rachmaninov playing in the background. Not a quick embrace among the DSS leaflets, just a focus on transactions that were causing problems. Every week these publications homed in on us and we dutifully filed them away with Lizzie occasionally wading through the welter of information and sorting out the few tiny paragraphs relevant to us. Sometimes we would get details of a new type of transaction (for example, Travel Insurance) with the worrying comment at the bottom of the new item circular: "For details *see Counters Bulletin 1996 No, 7.* Guess which issue of *Counters Bulletin* wasn't filed away.

We also had to contend with the secret service wing of the Post Office known officially as the mystery shoppers (come to think of it, a lot of our shoppers fitted that description). A spy posing as a customer would come in and ask a few challenging questions. The questions themselves should have given the game away - we didn't have many customers asking about restrictions on air parcels to the Central African Republic, or whether it was possible to order travellers' cheques in Jordanian Dinars.

The mystery shopper idea was disturbing and we hoped that organisations like the Environmental Health Department didn't take it up. Whatever their faults, Environmental Health Officers were generally up front. The Mystery Environmental Health Officer was a concept that *really* had us worried.

In one sense we mastered the post office very quickly but in another we never really mastered it at all. There were so many types of transaction and as we only faced some of them once or twice a year, we never really felt at ease with them. But we coped, and with increasing confidence brought this little bureaucratic monster to heel. To get rid of the miscellaneous piles of paper that were springing up all over the house, we bought a filing cabinet, and filled it with.... miscellaneous files. In the early days we were supported by what we thought of as our Post Office family - the offices in the neighbouring villages, our benign Visiting Officers, Head Office at Gloucester – and it was a real comfort to have such a sound local support system helping us through this administrative jungle.

As well as the shop and the post office, we also had the house to contend with. Harold had left the shop in good order but had done little to the house save putting hardboard over each attractive feature and painting walls and woodwork the same dull cream. The bathroom was downstairs which meant that anyone wwanting the loo in the middle of the night had to negotiate the burglar alarm before relief could be obtained. By rationalising our storage area, we found space for an upstairs bathroom. We then extended the kitchen, converted the loft, added a conservatory, built false walls and false floors, stripped woodwork and floorboards, and redecorated from top to bottom. You name it we were probably doing it - or thinking about it. And as we didn't have unlimited cash we were doing most of it ourselves. In addition, Lizzie took on the shop accounts and I started a job with the British Council that entailed 20 hours a week at home and two overseas trips a year. Lizzie was also running the home and being a mother and I was trying to see *my* two children - who then lived forty miles away - at least twice a week.

Phew! Yet I don't remember ever being rushed off our feet or even feeling particularly tired. Maybe it was the initial enthusiasm that generated an excess of adrenaline, or perhaps the stress-free nature of the lifestyle. Whatever the reason, it was all eminently manageable once we'd got over our teething troubles. During our first six months I even ran two teacher training courses for the British Council and wrote three - unaccepted - TV plays.

A lot of this couldn't have been achieved if we hadn't acquired the services of a wonderful assistant called Joyce Tucker. Joyce was with us all the time we ran the shop and appears frequently in this narrative. But even with Joyce's help, I'm still surprised how much we achieved in those early years. Ah, but we were young then. Or younger at any rate. Two years after taking over the property, our main refurbishments were finished and we had completed our apprenticeship. We knew the business (large parts of it), got on well with the customers (most of them), and felt that the decision to buy a village stores had been the right one. And with Poulton's other shop closing and bequeathing us newspapers and vegetables, business was suddenly booming.

But as an old friend in Khartoum used to say, beware hubris!

CHAPTER TWO

LEARNING THE HARD WAY

A Fly in the Ointment

High on the public's list of suspect professions are politicians, journalists and estate agents; (a firm of estate agents in Leicestershire was called Swindell and Trolloppe – and it was *still* successful!) While few shopkeepers would disagree with these perceptions, most would want to add a few of their own. Bankers and Environmental Health Officers would certainly find places in the top ten and in the light of our experience, accountants would be up there with them. I must add in fairness that our current accountant is among the highest specimens of humanity. Our first was among the lowest. I'm exaggerating, but not by much.

You already know that we came into the retail business totally green. We'd read books, been to meetings, looked at articles and inspected various premises and balance sheets but in terms of "hands on" experience, we were complete beginners. One thing we did know, however, was that we had to have an accountant. We were told to get one who was "hungry", drove a ten-year-old Skoda, and specialised in small businesses. Having little idea where to find such a person, we asked the bank manager.

Now our bank manager was a very nice man with a bedside manner that induced a bout of amnesia every time we saw him and made us forget his conduct of our affairs during the previous three years. Inaccurate investment advice and mishandling of our day-to-day banking had cost us several thousand pounds and he even admitted in writing that he had treated our affairs in a "somewhat cavalier fashion." Yet this was the man we approached to find us a suitable accountant in the Cirencester area. We must have been off our heads.

He came up with two names which, although we didn't know it at the time, were the names of the two biggest accountancy firms in the area. The one we chose was almost certainly the worse on the grounds that the other just had to have been better. The partner who looked after our affairs certainly wasn't hungry and didn't

31

drive a ten-year-old anything. All the bank manager had done was phone his colleagues in Cirencester or consult the yellow pages, either of which we could have done ourselves. We had asked him to find us a "suitable" accountant; he had ignored the word suitable.

His advice again proved very expensive. After nine months we had a VAT inspection and on seeing the size of our accountancy bills the inspector asked if we were running Sainsbury's. A phone call cost £25, a visit £40. Not many phone calls or visits were made. We looked askance at one bill which was itemised as

Meeting with Senior Partner: £x.00

Advice given at meeting: £y.00.

At this point we knew we were dealing with a master. Charging for the time taken to perform the service as well as for the service itself was an exciting new concept. This was obviously what he had meant at our first meeting when he enthused about "creative accounting". We wondered if *we* could work the same sleight of hand. Could I charge for a lesson and charge extra for what was taught in the lesson? Could we charge for serving a customer and charge extra for the goods bought? Unfortunately, those of us living in the real world don't have access to this financial licence but accountants seem able to charge what they like. We later discovered that the partner who handled our affairs was an evangelist. He had obviously never taken to heart the bit in the New Testament about camels and eyes of needles.

It was a few years before we came to our senses and changed to a user-friendly accountant recommended by a neighbouring shop. And what a contrast with the evangelist. He's a Christian for a start and gives without always counting the cost. When we left the evangelist and on the understanding that it wouldn't cost us an arm and a leg (we'd none left!) we asked him to finish off our accounts for that year. He assured us that the fee for the remainder of the work would be "nominal" as there were "just a few loose ends to tie up." Those loose ends cost almost as much as our new accountant charged for a whole year. In fairness, the evangelist was a partner in a large company and his fees included an element for secretaries, plush offices, an in-house magazine and investment advice, services that we didn't need and certainly couldn't afford. As far as our business was concerned he was just about the most unsuitable accountant we could have found.

Lizzie did the bookkeeping herself and I completed our VAT returns otherwise I dread to think what our bills would have been. I once thought up an appropriate slogan for our second accountant: "We pay you hundreds, you save us thousands." With our evangelical friend it was definitely the other way round.

Choosing an accountant was our first experience of learning the hard way, our first contact with the more hard-nosed aspects of the world of business. We were to have a few similar experiences down the years but at the start, our disappointments were more concerned with our own business and with one or two attempts

'YOUR ANTI VILLAGE SHOP INJECTION, MR GLUM....'

we made to increase trade. We'd taken over the shop in a surge of optimism. We had energy, enthusiasm, personality. What we didn't have was the necessary cynicism about human nature, or an understanding of the resistance that many residents had built up *against* using their shop, almost as if they'd been injected against it. The following are a few of the disappointments as we explored ways of offering new services to the village.

The Londis Promotion.

The biggest let down came during our first year and gave us some indication of the consistency of the brick wall we'd started beating our heads against. Londis organised a special promotion offering discounts on a range of items and providing advertising material. This was our first chance to promote the shop and we approached it with enthusiasm. We bought a lot of the discounted items, delivered leaflets to every house, plastered the shop windows with posters, and waited for the customers to roll in.

The trouble was they didn't. Our regulars took advantage of the special offers and we were pleased they benefited but this wasn't the point of the exercise. The Londis promotion didn't gain us a single new customer and we were left with whole boxes of items such as Flash and Ajax Liquid that took years to get rid of. It all got too much for Joyce and one day she accosted one notorious non-customer as she came in for stamps.

"Now, Mrs. Flay, what about buying some of our special offers?" Joyce said, thrusting a leaflet in her face. The woman flushed as she looked down the list.

"I don't think we use anything on this list," she stammered but Joyce was at her most acerbic.

"What," she snorted, "not even bog rolls?"

The woman spluttered and left. She would have been wise to have bought a toilet roll to confirm that she had at least one human characteristic.

The Christmas Wine Order

Christmas in the shop was a time of mixed feelings. There was the extra post office work to deal with - parcels of all sizes and to all destinations, the extra stamp orders, the last posting dates - the worry about whether to order extra stock and if so what and how much. But on the credit side there were mince pies, decorations, Christmas cards, carols playing, not to mention a few days off. We always felt we should offer the village something a bit different at Christmas and before our second Christmas we tried another initiative.

Harold had bequeathed an excellent vintner who came every six weeks or so to replenish our stock. A few months before Christmas 1987, he suggested trying to get the village to buy its Christmas wine from the shop. The idea was appealing to us and after a little publicity the response was sufficiently encouraging for us to give it a try.

Delivery was promised a few days before Christmas and on 20th December we made our first enquiry. We were told not to worry as everything was under control and the wine would be delivered "any day now." Two days passed and customers were beginning to ask when they could collect their wine. No wine had as yet materialised and we began to detect a problem.

By the twenty-third, we were really anxious. The vintners by now were less reassuring and we began to have serious doubts whether the wine would arrive at all. The irate phone calls from customers who by this time hoped to have cracked a couple of bottles made Christmas Eve - when the wine still hadn't arrived - an absolute nightmare.

"How does Tuesday 28th sound?" a beleaguered transport officer asked me when I phoned him.

Tuesday 28th? For a Christmas wine order? Suddenly our whole credibility as shopkeepers was on the line and for a venture that might net us fifty quid if we were lucky. We looked frantically at the wine we had in stock. Would La Rochette be an acceptable substitute for the Claret we'd ordered? Could we pass off Liebfraumilch as an Australian chardonnay? The situation had driven us to the edge.

Around eight o'clock - long after we'd closed for the night - the order arrived, the driver sweating buckets and implying we had no right to drag him out on Christmas Eve. We loaded the wine into the car and delivered it to the customers. The village and its shopkeepers breathed a heavy sigh of relief and we vowed never again. Our first attempt at providing Poulton with its Christmas wine was also our last.

Five small loaves and.....?

The word "fish" has several connotations - a command, a description, one of the blood sports not under the threat of legislation, a bone of contention between Britain, Iceland and Spain, a substitute for a more expressive but less acceptable expletive.

To us the word revives memories of another attempt to increase trade by offering the village something new. We hadn't learnt the lesson of the Christmas wine and when the son of one of our customers became a fishmonger, we decided to add fresh fish to our range of products. (In passing, the fishmonger's parents started sending smoked salmon to America by post showing an unprecedented faith in the Royal Mail's overseas service. The observation "This service stinks" might for once have been meant literally).

Anyway, we went ahead with the fresh fish venture with customers placing their orders during the week and collecting them on Friday. That at least was the theory. In practice, delivery after delivery either failed to materialise or was completely wrong. I was reminded of the reaction of an irate messing officer during my National Service days who suddenly yelled at the cook corporal "What we need in this mess is not a bloody cook. It's five small loaves, two small fishes and Jesus Christ!"Lizzie was frequently tempted to yell something similar – the two small fishes would have been particularly welcome - and for months she would pale at the very mention of fish. Most customers were sympathetic but for some it gained us a reputation for unreliability and one actually accused us of sharp practice. He ordered a pound of cod and when his order arrived - he was one of the lucky ones - it weighed a few ounces over. I tried to tease him about bigger codpieces but this chap wasn't noted for his sense of humour and when Lizzie gave him the bill, he virtually accused her of conning him into buying more than he wanted. He left in a huff and never set foot in the shop again so the episode did have its advantages.

The young fishmonger seemed to suffer not only from bad organisational sense but also from the most appalling luck. While his business was still in its infancy and at his busiest time of year, he wrote off his only two vans by crashing one into the other on an icy road. I happened to be passing at the time and as I gave him a lift back to Poulton and listened to his tale of woe, I reflected sadly that here was another embryonic business about to bite the dust.

Several years on and his business is turning over millions and supplying fresh fish to a third of the country as well as being featured on *The Food Programme*. I can spot a loser when I see one! He didn't supply Poulton Post Office for very long and obviously our dealings with him didn't reflect his overall business ability. Perhaps the village shop was too small for him. Perhaps he had bigger fish to fry (ugh).

But we gave him up before he gave us up. The orders dwindled and the small amount of extra business - as with so many new ventures - wasn't worth the hassle. It was another point on the learning curve and at least got rid of one unpleasant customer.

The Copper Relief

After our years in Africa, we had many friends still languishing in the ex-colonies, people who were soldiering on in unpromising jobs instead of seeing the light and buying a post office in the Cotswolds.

One such was Peter James. At a late age and with the help of Veronica, his "little piranha of a wife"(his description), Peter had begotten a family and we reckoned he would be about seventy before his paternal duties were discharged. The great things about Peter were his eternal optimism and his never-ending chain of moneymaking schemes.

Peter and Veronica visited us in 1986 when Peter produced his latest money-spinner, a copper relief crafted by a friend in Kenya. Even the best copper reliefs are no things of beauty and this grotesque depiction of Tower Bridge was in no sense the best copper relief. For some reason, Peter had categorised our shop as a good retail outlet. "It's not exactly an impulse buy, is it?" we reflected as he set the price at £350. "People aren't likely to pop in for a packet of tea bags and say as an afterthought, "And I'll have one of those, please."

"But isn't there a lot of people with money in these parts?" he asked.

Yes there is Peter, a lot of people with *lots* of money. But we knew just how hard it was to get them to spend it.

Which brings us to the Reverend Richard Needle. The Reverend Needle was something of a legend around Poulton, a man who kept his Christian heart well-hidden beneath a bigoted facade. Only two people in the village took the *Church Times* and one day the two were in the shop together. " Richard" I said to Needle, "let me introduce you to the other Christian in the village." "You mean the *only* Christian in the village," Needle snorted. "People have accused me of many things but I've never before been accused of being a Christian."

"But your dog collar?" I protested.

"A rather good disguise."

I tried to interest him in the copper relief. He was fascinated by it - as all men of the cloth should be fascinated by true ugliness. I think he recognised the devil's work when he saw it and there was a glint in his eye as he offered to buy it.

"But only if I can get it with my supermarket stamps," he added, knowing this would upset me. I finally got a promise that he would buy it for the wall of his fourth loo.

"How many loos have you got?" I asked.

"One and a bit" he replied and left me to make of that what I would.

He never did buy it and after a few weeks - it seemed like years - we removed it from the shop. Village shop users are a small band of loyal or desperate people. One thing the episode of the copper relief proved conclusively, however, was that it is indeed difficult to get them to part with large sums of money.

Either that or they have impeccable taste.

Elf Meadow.

Although this episode isn't directly related to the shop, it was another of our early disappointments and so I've decided to include it. A few months after we moved in, the petrol station over the road closed and eight houses were built on the adjoining land. Eight new houses opposite the shop! We rubbed our hands and looked forward to a substantial increase in trade. But the anti-shop jabs must have been part of the contract and far from giving us a substantial increase in trade, the new estate gave us hardly any trade at all.

On a lighter note, Elf Meadow isn't mentioned in Poulton's official history, *A World in a Grain of Sand*. I hope the history is updated before too long. If not, I can see future historians engaging in many speculations about the origin of the name and imagining pixies in fairy dells and all kinds of magical and dark scenarios.

The truth, sadly, is far less exotic. The road was named after the product sold at the service station that preceded it on the site - Elf petrol.

So the first steep rise on our learning curve ended and by 1988 we had learned at least two things: changing our accountant was a matter of priority, and nothing short of a royal decree would get most villagers to use the shop. Initiatives were disappointing and expecting an increase in turnover from new housing was a waste of time. All that could be hoped for was a slight improvement at the margins. In fairness, the Copper Relief wasn't really an initiative and the fresh fish and Christmas wine orders failed through the unreliability of the supplies. But we now had a better idea of what might work and what probably wouldn't. We also knew that we would have to rely on a small percentage of the village to keep us viable.

Then in the early months of 1988, the other shop in the village closed. We inherited the newspaper business, increased our market for fruit and vegetables and saw a substantial increase in the sales of other products. We achieved the surge in trade we were looking for more by luck than judgement. It took us a little longer to get round to changing our accountant.

CHAPTER TWO

A LIFE IN THE DAY OF A VILLAGE SHOPKEEPER

Dealing with the public could be as trying as it was satisfying particularly as many of our customers were old people with diminishing faculties. Like Mrs Cauldron, an old woman in her eighties who was buying her daily bottle of sherry one morning when her daughter came in.

"At the sherry again, mother," the daughter said and the old woman jumped.

"What's it to do with you?" she asked venomously. "Anyway, it's not alcoholic."

When Mrs Cauldron had gone, the daughter asked if we'd mind not selling her mother so much sherry. "It's not that I begrudge it her," she explained. "It's just that when I come home from work I can't get any sense out of her. She's three sheets to the wind."

When I suggested that it might be difficult to say no to Mrs Cauldron who was a very strongwilled woman, she pointed to a grape drink called Schloer. "Give her a bottle of that. She won't know the difference."

So the next time Mrs Cauldron asked for sherry, I did as her daughter had suggested. A lorry driver standing behind her looked hard at me and I knew exactly what he was thinking. "Village shopkeeper taking advantage of an old lady. Giving her

Schloer and charging her for sherry. Cut their grannies' throats for a fiver these jokers." But with Mrs Cauldron happily deceived according to her daughter's wishes, I could hardly disabuse him. So are lies circulated and myths established.

Anyway, off went Mrs Cauldron with her bottle of Schloer and when I next saw her daughter I asked how our little subterfuge was going.

"Terrible," she said. "She finishes the Schloer then goes to the pub."

* * * * * * * * * *

"Watch it," Joyce whispered to me later the same morning. "Cordelia's put three pairs of tights in her bag."

Not that Cordelia was an inveterate shoplifter. It was just that her mind had started to go. Sadly it was the beginning of Alzheimer's. Cordelia lived with her son about a mile outside Poulton and even when her illness was quite advanced, she remained a delightful woman and came to the shop every day with her carer. After a time her son became concerned about her account, both its size and the items on it. He was amazed, for example, to discover that his ageing mother was buying Tampax. But it was the daily bottle of whisky that really concerned him. "She drinks it like water" he explained. "Give her a bottle of wine instead. It's cheaper and won't do her as much harm. And," (shades of Mrs Cauldron's daughter) "she'll never know the difference."

When it became clear that she did know the difference, refusing to accept wine while we had whisky on the shelves, he hit on another ruse.

"When you see her coming, hide all the whisky. Tell her you've sold it."

So that's what we did. The next time the carer's car drew up, we whipped all the whisky to the back of the shop out of sight. Cordelia came in, her usual charming self, and asked for her regular bottle. When we said we were out of stock, her smile faded and a steely glint came into her eyes. "That's funny," she said, "You had such a lot yesterday. Are you sure you're not hiding it?"

Like Mrs Cauldron she wasn't to be fooled. Old people may lose many of their faculties but the faculty to track down booze isn't one of them. When it came to her alcohol, Cordelia changed from an absentminded old shuffler into a human lie detector spotting the merest hint of dissemblance like a supercharged Miss Marples.

As Cordelia's disease worsened, we had to keep a constant eye on her as she wandered round the shop slipping various items into her bag. On the day Joyce alerted me to the three pairs of tights, I recorded the other things in her basket and then casually asked if she had any tights.

"Of course I have tights," she barked.

I asked if I could see them.

"What here?" she queried. 'Oh all right, if you insist." and smiling sweetly she lifted up her skirt. I hastily explained that those weren't the tights I had in mind, left the others in her bag and marked down three pairs anyway. Why had no one warned us about such things before we came into the business? Dealing with demented old ladies had never been discussed at the various seminars we attended.

* * * * * * * * * *

"Two rashers of bacon."

I looked up and, seeing the sour face of Mrs Beech peering over the counter, steeled myself for a lengthy transaction. Harold had warned me that Mrs Beech's two rashers of bacon were one of the trials of the week but I thought he must be exaggerating. Two rashers of bacon are after all two rashers of bacon.

To most people, perhaps, but not to Mrs Beech. She drew distinctions between rashers like a Greenlander identifying different kinds of snow. The line between too much fat and too little fat was a fine one and easily crossed by anyone not well-versed in the intricacies of the subject. After some deliberation, I weighed the two rashers which to my untrained eye looked the best only to hear them immediately pronounced unacceptable. "Too much fat" she said hardly giving them a glance. I put them back in the fridge and weighed two more.

"Two heavy," she barked. "It'll cost the earth."

I weighed a further two, which she grudgingly accepted – until I told her the price.

"You've really put your prices up. This bacon is much dearer than when the last people were here."

Between clenched teeth, I explained that the bacon prices hadn't changed and she shook her head. "Well I don't know. It seems impossible to get two decent rashers of bacon in this shop any-more. I suppose I'd better have the first two you showed me."

Smiling fixedly, I was trying to remember which the first two were when Lizzie emerged from the house. Mrs Beech looked at her with concern.

"You're not going out, are you?"

Lizzie said she was, whereupon Mrs Beech shook her head and jerked her thumb in my direction.

"I wouldn't be happy leaving *him* in charge."

On my knees, trying to find two acceptable rashers of bacon from a selection that all looked the same, I came within an ace of wrapping every single rasher round Mrs Beech's head.

*   *   *   *   *   *   *   *   *   *

I'd finally dispatched Mrs Beech, still muttering about the price of her two rashers and how shopkeeping standards had fallen, when to my horror I saw Miss Cocker shuffling towards the shop. Miss Cocker was the most charismatic of all our customers though perhaps charismatic isn't *quite* the word I want. She certainly had her own aura but it was hardly the kind to inspire or enchant.

Quite simply Miss Cocker stank to high heaven. And this wasn't an intermittent she's-been-eating-garlic or he-hasn't-washed-his-armpits smell. This was a smell that all the rosewater baths in the world couldn't get rid of, a straight-through-the-skin-down-to-the- bones smell, the result of living in a small cottage with an assortment of dogs that had been allowed to foul the place for as long as anyone could remember. The smell was in her clothes, in her flesh, in her person. She always wore a little rouge and a little lipstick and seemed oblivious to the effect she had on people. When she'd left, the smell remained and we used to dread an environmental health officer following her into the shop. He would never have believed the smell wasn't an intrinsic part of the establishment and who could have blamed him? The local builder, Frank Pitt, was one of the few people who ever entered her house and his devotion went way beyond the call of duty. She'd phone to say she'd fallen out of bed; Frank would go and pick her up. She wanted her toilet seat changed; Frank would change it and take on sundry other mouth-watering assignments. Light bulbs, television repairs, plumbing problems, Frank waded in where others (including ourselves) feared to tread and came back with stories of living conditions that would have disgraced a pigsty.

But no one else would go near the place. A friend who Frank asked to repair Miss Cocker's TV set almost passed out as he entered. He whipped the TV away and gave it Frank to return. "Don't you ever do anything like that to me again," he said.

I went in only once, when Miss Cocker was in hospital and Frank and his boys had been cleaning up. They'd been working for several days yet the place still looked unfit for human habitation.

"I see what you mean about the smell," I said, screwing up my nose.

"What do you mean?" said Frank. "The place has been fumigated. The smell's gone!"

So even on the best of days, the sight of Miss Cocker entering the shop wasn't particularly welcome and this was definitely not the best of days. I usually bolted into the house and left Lizzie or Joyce to cope but Lizzie was out and Joyce had gone home. I took a deep breath and wondered how long I could hold it. I felt distinctly uncharitable particularly as Miss Cocker wasn't at all a difficult customer. Friendly and amusing, she would chat intelligently about this and that even at times assuming a somewhat flirtatious air, though that line of thought really is too dreadful to contemplate.

Anyway, as she entered I beat a hasty retreat into the post office and stayed there until she'd left, maintaining just enough contact to hand over her pension. Call me a coward if you like (in fact I don't know what else you'd call me) but after Mrs Cauldron, Cordelia and Mrs Beech, dealing with Miss Cocker was very nearly the last straw.

Then to put the tin hat on a perfect day, that nice Mr Minnow came in with his post. He always cut it fine but today he came in even later than usual with his disarming smile and two large parcels to post to his son who was with the army in Germany. The postman explained that as it was already half-past five he couldn't wait for the parcels to be processed and made as if to leave.

So much for our pleasant, benign customer. The genie of rage exploded from the bottle with a vengeance. Mr Minnow started ranting like a man possessed, cursing the "wasters" at the Post Office who were "always on strike", who wouldn't put themselves out for "our boys overseas", and more and more of the same ilk.

Hang on, I thought. We're talking Germany not the Congo, and Germany 1986 was hardly Germany 1940. And "our boys" weren't conscripts but professional soldiers, in the army by choice.

He raged round the shop, frightening off other customers and behaving in such an aggressive way towards the postman that I eventually asked him to stop. At this he turned on *me* with his fists raised accusing me of being a joke and not taking either the job or "our boys" seriously.

Just then, one of our delivery drivers came in, six foot six and built like the proverbial outhouse.

"Need any help?" he asked with a hint of menace and seeing the two of us towering over him, Mr Minnow obviously didn't fancy the odds. He stormed out taking his parcels with him and we never saw him again.

Minutes later I closed the shop and sank wearily into a chair, sorely tempted to take a leaf out of Mrs Cauldron's book and pop to the pub for a large sherry. How difficult it was on such a day to abide by the age old dictum that the customer is always right.

PART THREE

TALKING SHOP

CHAPTER 1

MINDING OUR OWN BUSINESS

The innocents abroad phase soon passed; it didn't take us long to find our feet and enjoy the thought that after many years working for other organisations we were at last "minding our own business".

This of course is what all shopkeepers do unless they can afford to pay someone to mind it for them. But village shopkeepers spend a lot of their time minding other people's business as well. The shop is the centre of the village and we were always among the first to be told if there was anything newsworthy to report – Mrs Smith had died, a Neighbourhood Watch meeting was being held in the village hall, the new residents in Elf Meadow were called Jones, Mr X had been seen coming out of Mrs Y's house at six in the morning, and so on. Apart from what people *chose* to tell us (and this could be anything from their partner's taste in soup to the reasons why their marriage was breaking down), we had a knowledge of people's finances, prejudices and tastes that we were honour-bound to keep to ourselves. In the case of information gained from Post Office business, we were more than honour-bound - all Post Office employees are governed by the Official Secrets Act.

We were fascinated more by the *unofficial* secrets our position gave us access to and the foibles of human nature they represented. We knew for instance what people drank and could hazard a reasonable guess as to how much. We knew what and how much they smoked, whether they were worried about their weight, what newspaper they read - tabloid or broadsheet, right wing or left wing. We knew if (like us) they were habitually late paying bills, the level of income support they received, the balance of their National Savings Account, whether they allowed their children vast quantities of junk food, even when they had anything that might be called an addiction. We knew where they had contacts overseas and how often they wrote to them, even in one instance whether they were claiming benefit they weren't entitled to. But in most of this we were sworn to silence.

47

There's a fine line between showing a natural curiosity about human nature and being too interested in somebody else's business. One customer interpreted our completion of the formalities of a National Savings transaction as being "bloody nosey" and never set foot in the shop again. Until the day after we left, that is. Then she was back, arranging a paper delivery and saying how nice it would be to have a newspaper with her breakfast again. "Nose", "cut off" and "face" are words that come to mind.

There was at least one other occasion when we unwittingly gave offence, although this time we had no idea who the customer was. We learned about it when the Post Office conducted a survey to assess the public's opinion of post offices and their staff. The questionnaires contained several categories - politeness, privacy when queuing, waiting times, availability of leaflets, staff's ability to provide information - which could all be classed as "very satisfactory", "satisfactory", "quite satisfactory" or "not at all satisfactory". The completed questionnaires were then placed in a box in the post office and were available for us to look at. We were classed as "very satisfactory" or "satisfactory" for all categories on all questionnaires.

Except one. One customer had ticked "Not at all satisfactory" for every category. Including "Availability of Leaflets". Now I'm quite prepared to admit that we may - occasionally - have been rude, inept and ignorant but it's difficult to remember a time when we didn't have a superabundance of leaflets. Unless the customer was looking for a leaflet that we didn't know existed - "Health Care for Polar Explorers" for example, or "Rabies and the Village Shop Customer" - this criticism was just a little over the top.

As the questionnaires were anonymous, we had no idea who we had offended to such an extent, or why. We could only echo George Bernard Shaw's comment after a performance of one of his plays when, after rapturous applause, there was a solitary boo. " I agree with you, sir," Shaw said turning in the direction of the boo. "I agree with you completely. But...what are we two against so many?"

But minding your own business means you can never walk away when problems arise and even shopkeepers who operate minimal opening hours are still on duty twenty four hours a day. Problems occur even in the most organised of businesses - and we were never the most organised of businesses. Some of the problems were beyond our control. Not even our questionnaire critic could have blamed us when the property was struck by lightning and we lost several circuits as well as all our electronic equipment. Then again, although we took all reasonable precautions, our security budget didn't run to warning us when armed bandits were heading our way. But when the freezer was accidentally switched off (twice) and we lost our supply of frozen food, we couldn't seriously blame it on anything but carelessness. Anymore than when we lost the keys to the shop safe.

When Harold handed over the business, he also handed over two bunches of keys, one for the post office, the other for the shop. On the post office ring were one long key for the safe and three or four small keys. On the shop ring were a Yale (for the post office door), two medium-sized keys (for the shop safe and the shop door) and two or three small keys. In twelve years, we never found out what the small keys (on either ring) were for yet never had the confidence to throw them away. All this should tell you as much about us as it does about the keys.

Neither of us has a particularly good record with keys, either keeping them or using them. One of the first things we bought for our future together was a fretwork key holder. It fell to pieces before we had a chance to use it. I remember my ex- wife turning the air of Malawi blue the day I went off in a friend's car with our only set of car keys. On the day of Lizzie's parents' golden wedding party, we were halfway to Nottinghamshire before we realised that not only had neither of us locked the front door, we hadn't even closed it. We had left the house, the shop and the post office open to the four winds. We phoned Joyce who was most amused and went and locked it for us. So you can see that we treat keys a bit like the bank manager treated our finances, in a "somewhat cavalier fashion".

However, when we lost the shop keys, it seemed this slapdash approach had landed us in trouble. In the safe was the cash box with a week's takings and the benefit book we kept as a surety for a customer's credit. When it became clear that this wasn't just another of our periodic misplacements and the keys might well have been stolen, we changed the lock on the shop door and asked Joyce's husband to use his welding equipment to break into the safe. Watching him work, I wondered if he hadn't missed his vocation. The safe was "cracked" in no time and we hauled the cash box and the benefit book through the hole in the door.

The hole was still there years later when we left. Oh and the keys finally turned up in the mortgage file, supporting the claim that a badly organised filing cabinet is the best hiding place in the world.

So we had problems with lost keys, with freezers de-frosting, with lightning homing in on our business, and even with robbers targeting our friendly little post office. We also had the occasional flood in the back store, mice nibbling away at our stock, and wastage through over-ordering and punitive sell-by dates. But although these things loomed large at the time, most of them were minor blips on the smooth surface of the business we had bought and the lifestyle that came with it. It was only when bureaucracy began to bite and the environmental health regime bore down that we began to have real misgivings but these came much later.

CHAPTER TWO

CONFIDENCE TRICKS.

Don't touch the door knob. It's got twenty thousand volts running through it! **(Peter Sellars)**

The alarm bells started ringing as soon as he entered the shop. Dark and swarthy, black hair plastered to his head, viva zapata moustache, dark glasses, black shirt, white raincoat tightly belted, mean-looking and shifty-eyed, he bundled his way past a slight woman with two children in tow and came to the post office. And

SPOT THE CROOK....

didn't we detect an Eastern European accent when he spoke? I looked at the name on the benefit book. John Reginald Smith of Ampney Crucis indeed! Within seconds I was on the phone to the Fraud Hotline ready to claim my fifty pounds reward or whatever they were offering these days. The gangster-like figure lurking the other side of the anti-bandit screen turned out to be .... John Reginald Smith of Ampney Crucis.

It was the slight woman with the two children in tow who defrauded us.

In the seminars we attended and the books we read, our attention was drawn to how vulnerable shopkeepers are to the petty criminal and, while no one suggested we went to the lengths of the Peter Sellars character above, we were encouraged to treat the possibility of theft very seriously. The Post Office warned us about fraud and robberies; retailing organisations drew attention to such things as staff dishonesty, shoplifting, and bad debts. The question of staff dishonesty never arose. We trusted all the people who worked for us and never had any reason to suspect this trust was misplaced. In addition, during our twelve years in charge, although we substantially increased our credit facilities, we had only one bad debt. But we were still encouraged to treat customers - particularly strangers - with suspicion and realised after a while that, to parody the old Peter Cook and Dudley Moore sketch, this was no way to run a ballroom. The shop had to be a welcoming place where people were greeted as friends and deemed trustworthy until they proved otherwise.

Actually it was salesmen rather than petty criminals who tried to take advantage of us in the early days. They hear on the grapevine that a shop is under new management and descend like vultures. One of them persuaded us to buy £60 worth of shoelaces. "You won't regret it," he said as he pocketed the cheque. "Sell like hot cakes they will." We still had most of those "hot cakes" when we left twelve years later.

Some of the most persistent salesmen were those selling video surveillance and offering systems to buy or rent. As they gave us the sales pitch, three things became clear. Firstly any possible savings could never justify the sums involved. "You'd be surprised how much gets nicked from a shop like this," one of them said. Well, yes, if it covered the weekly rent he quoted we *would* have been surprised. Secondly, video surveillance in such a small shop was unnecessary. The layout ensured that almost all areas were in view and those that weren't housed things like cleaning products and pet food, items unlikely to tempt even the most dedicated shoplifter. And thirdly, the presence of video screens would have run counter to the atmosphere of friendliness we were trying to create. We could hardly expect the village to treat us as friends and feel welcome in what we characterised as "their" shop while installing a system which said in effect " Big Brother is Watching."

So video surveillance was out and we never regretted it. To our knowledge there was only one occasion when it might have helped and that was just after we started selling hot pies. Heating the pies involved going to the microwave in the kitchen and staying there for perhaps a minute and a half to ensure the pies were hot enough. Most customers found them, if anything, too hot.

Except one. He always ordered a large Cornish pasty and liked it hot enough to take the skin off his mouth. "Two minutes" I'd say.

"Two and a half" he'd reply. I'd disappear into the kitchen and emerge a few minutes later with a pasty I could hardly hold.

After a few weeks something clicked. It eventually got through even to my retarded sense of suspicion that the pasties I was handing over would take the roof off his mouth. Halfway to the kitchen, I crept back and watched in disbelief as he went behind the counter and slipped a half bottle of whisky into the pocket of his overalls. His action was all the more astonishing as there was another customer in the shop.

I heated his pasty and as I gave it to him asked if he intended paying for the whisky. He feigned innocence until I threatened to phone the police when he put the whisky on the counter and made a hasty departure. I wasn't quite sure what to do and eventually did nothing.

I realise now I was wrong and that there were several reasons I should have reported him. First, he had broken the law, second stealing whisky and perhaps drinking it in the afternoons suggested that he had a drink problem that needed addressing. But most importantly, he was the driver of a school bus and was clearly unsuitable for such a responsible job.

But our instances of observed theft amounted to no more than the one above. We may have lost some stock to petty pilfering - boys will be boys after all - but what the eye didn't see, the heart didn't grieve over. And it was never enough to make a hole in our profits.

Fraud was a different matter but even then the instances were comparatively rare. The Post Office set up several fraud hotlines - for Girobank fraud, National Savings fraud, Benefit fraud and so on but these things don't normally concern village postmasters. We were on first name terms with most of our customers and contrary to what we are occasionally led to believe by the media, the public by and large is honest. Whenever a pension book was dropped outside the post office - sometimes with that week's money tucked inside - it was invariably handed in, often by a stranger. When customers we didn't know came to the post office to cash orders or withdraw money, we naturally checked their identification. Most people were happy to comply but a few thought we were impugning their honesty. We explained that the checks were for their protection and most of them saw reason.

The worst thing about being defrauded is the feeling of gullibility. When Iago described Othello as being "of a free and open nature who thinks men honest who do but seem to be so" he could have been describing me with Lizzie not far behind. So when someone took advantage of our "free and open natures" we felt bemused. And angry. Angrier even than when we suffered an armed robbery which at least had a brutal honesty about it.

There is something despicable about fraudsters. They take advantage of innocence and vulnerability, striking at what they see as easy targets - and a village post office in a sleepy part of the Cotswolds is seen as the easiest of targets. Both of us suffered independently from people drawing cash on stolen benefit books. On each occasion we realised too late and tried to note the fraudster's car number. The first time it was impossible as the two women who defrauded us had parked well out of sight. On the second occasion, the car as well as the order book turned out to be stolen. We also cashed a dud cheque during our first six months and just after the Post Office had started cashing other banks' cheques. The chequebook wasn't stolen - there was just no money in the account. The fraudster had been on a tour of Cotswold post offices cashing fifty pounds at each and no one, not even experienced counters staff, had bothered to punch the date in the back of his chequebook - a safeguard against cashing more than one cheque on the same day. We wrote to the Post Office pleading inexperience and they agreed to go halves. These days we'd probably have to pay it all.

If we failed to follow the correct procedure - insisting on a guarantee card, writing the number on the back of the cheque, checking the signature and punching the cheque book calendar - we deserved to be held responsible. There was one instance, however, when we did all these things but the bank still returned the cheque. It turned out that both chequebook and card were stolen. We wrote to the bank asking them to honour the £50 guarantee pointing out the amount of extra business the guarantee generated. We also explained that the similarity between the signatures on the card and on the cheque would have fooled anyone who wasn't a handwriting expert. For once the bank reacted sympathetically and honoured the cheque. We look back on this as a unique experience, an occasion when we had reason to be grateful to a bank.

But these instances apart, our time in the post office was mercifully free of dishonesty and proved what we said before, that the bulk of the population is honest. We would encourage other shopkeepers, while taking all reasonable precautions, to class customers as honest until they prove otherwise rather than the other way round. As Dr. Johnson remarked, "It is happier to be sometimes cheated than not to trust."

In twelve years we cashed about 120,000 benefits, issued 10,000 tax discs, and sold £120,000 of stamps. Around £1,000,000 passed through our till of which £250,000 was in credit sales. In that time we had perhaps half a dozen cases of benefit fraud, four dud cheques and one bad debt. I think we can tentatively conclude that our customers were honest.

CHAPTER 3

GENTLEMEN OF THE PRESS

Reading someone else's newspaper is like sleeping with someone else's wife. Nothing seems to be precisely in the right place and when you find what you are looking for, it is not clear how to respond to it. **(Malcolm Bradbury)**

In 1988, as Harold had predicted, the other shop in the village closed down. The owners, Margaret and Philip Edwards, had reached retirement age and couldn't sell the shop as a going concern. They had been running it all their lives and were archetypal shopkeepers. But the halcyon days of Edwards's store had long gone. It was off the main road and with no passing trade or post office salary, their profits must have been slim indeed. Eventually they bowed to the inevitable and offered us the one lucrative aspect of their business, the newspapers.

We received the offer with mixed feelings. It would mean much earlier mornings and another adjustment to our lifestyle. But profits on newspapers are considerable and we couldn't afford to refuse. Margaret taught us the ropes, giving clear explanations as to what paper was delivered to which house and where each customer lived. She and Philip had delivered to the neighbouring villages as well in their old Austin Maxi but we decided that if the newspapers were to be tolerable, we would have to employ paperboys and restrict deliveries to Poulton.

So newspapers entered our lives and my routine was changed forever. I say *my* routine as Lizzie maintained from the start that she would have nothing to do with any activity at such an unearthly hour. The newspaper business was my baby. I committed myself to organising the morning paper rounds and from February 1988 until September 1998, I never stayed in bed after 6.15 except on the few panic-stricken occasions when there was a power cut in the night and the radio alarm had failed.

All newspapers and most magazines were supplied on a "sale or return" basis and I left the business of sorting out the returns to my teenage daughter. At the start, the unsold copies were returned once a week and by Saturday there was a considerable pile. She would complete the returns lists and then dump the whole lot into a cornflake box. This had been going on for a few months when Lizzie got a phone call from the woman at the wholesalers who processed the returns.

"Does Mr. Russell think I'm *TARZAN?*" was her challenging opening before she made a plea for the returns to be packed in smaller bundles. A few weeks later we received a list of instructions on processing returns, restricting the size of bundles, banning the use of boxes and insisting on all bundles being tied securely. Now I see every newsagent in the land following the same procedure. I could be wrong but I have a feeling that my daughter's predilection for cornflake boxes coupled with the processor's inability to handle them resulted in a new national strategy for newspaper returns.

Every morning, we received newspapers of various styles and shades of opinion catering for the whole spectrum of cultural and political tastes. I used to believe that a person's choice of paper was an indication of their political bias but then there would have to be a newspaper that represented the views of the National Front, and there isn't - not even the *Sun* or the *Telegraph* at their worst. Thinking back to my childhood, I remember Uncle Alf - a dyed-in-the-wool Labour supporter - taking the *Daily Express*, presumably because he looked for things in his newspaper other than its political bias. Difficult though it may be for the politically-minded to believe, many people are turned off by politics. As Spike Milligan said during one election campaign. "One of these days the "don't knows" will get in and then where will we be."

But we still enjoyed speculating what their choice of newspaper revealed about people's attitudes. If one household, for example, took the *Telegraph* and the *Mail*, we assumed, perhaps wrongly, that the *Telegraph* was for the man, the *Mail* for the "little woman".

What we felt beyond reasonable doubt was that such a household was quite likely to vote Tory.

People buy newspapers for a variety of reasons. Many buy them for the television guide, some for the bingo cards, some for the naked starlets, many men exclusively for the sport, some for the fashion, the travel, the investment advice, the scandal, the horoscopes, some even to nurture their sense of outrage (which is why I occasionally read the letters page of the *Telegraph.*)

The quote by Malcolm Bradbury at the beginning of this chapter is compelling but misleading. Presumably one sleeps with somebody else's wife (or husband) for pleasure rather than curiosity whereas from the irate phone calls we received when deliveries had gone awry, it was clear that most people derive no pleasure at all from reading someone else's newspaper. A better analogy would be finding yourself in bed with someone you don't remotely fancy, as I'm sure any *Telegraph* reader who has ever received a *Guardian* would confirm. On the other hand, just as some people change their spouses, so others change their newspapers. Many were seduced when Rupert Murdoch reduced the price of the *Times* in a bid to encroach on the *Independent* and *Telegraph*. markets. He made no impression on the *Guardian* which suggests that Guardian readers are made of sterner stuff and won't sell their souls to the Australian-born devil for a few pence a week.

Newspaper people occupy the world of early mornings when most people are still tucked up in bed. They share this world with early morning broadcasters at the time when the World Service becomes Radio 4 and *Farming Today* deals with issues that no one, apart from farmers, are aware of. How could they be when they are broadcast at a time when only lunatics, insomniacs or newsagents are likely to hear them? It was a world I also shared with the cat and the dog as well as the occasional passing optimist who, seeing the light on in the shop, asked for directions. My jobs were to check the delivery and put up the rounds in time for the boys to deliver them before they caught the school bus. On the odd occasions I had to do a round myself, I'd be fully dressed otherwise it was dressing gown and slippers. On Mondays, the papers were easy to deal with - no magazines, no inserts. On Saturdays it was an epic, with supplements proliferating and the broadsheets engaged in an ongoing rivalry to see who could destroy the most rain forests.

As I checked my supplies, I would discover as likely as not that the packers at W.H. Smith had got them wrong. What Basil Fawlty was to hotel management, W.H. Smith are to newspaper wholesaling. For the thirteenth time this month - today was the fourteenth - they'd have buggered up my order. Two *Mirrors* short, three *Telegraphs* down and no *Mails* at all, just the daily example of inefficiency from what I genuinely believed was the most inefficient wholesaling organisation in the history of the world.

Meanwhile as complaints were being registered with an unresponsive wholesaler, in different parts of the village two adolescents were yawning and struggling out of bed. They pulled on tracksuits and waterproofs, listened to the rain buffeting against their windows then cycled off along watery streets to where the newspaper bags were waiting. On the worst mornings, I would look at the weather and feel stabs of guilt. Out in that for £10 a week. They must be mad and I must be evil to the core. How could I, a firm believer in human rights, a man whose father was a leading light in the Trades Union movement when it was still both democratic and influential, subject young boys to conditions that would have shamed a Victorian mill owner? I would remind myself that the paper rounds were incidental; what I was actually doing was offering a course in character-building (see the following chapter). Suitably reassured, I would take two cups of tea and the *Independent* back to bed.

When the phone rang in the early mornings, nine times out of ten it would be a complaint about the papers. Frequently the complaint was justified as it was another mistake either by me, the paper boys, or W.H. Smith, but I found it amazing how apoplectic people could get about their newspapers. One woman virtually accused me of robbing her of £50,000 because her scratch card was missing.

There was one old couple, gentle and polite people, who brought to mind the saying about butter not melting in their mouths.

Until something went wrong with their papers.

They had two daily papers and failure to deliver them correctly was close to a capital offence. Listening to the man ranting in the background as his wife phoned and reported a missing *Sun* I could almost imagine a torture chamber for bungling newsboys and shopkeepers at the back of their house with the slogan "We have ways of making you deliver the newspapers correctly," hanging on the door.

"Where is my *Sun*?" the woman would say.

"Sorry, Mrs Shine, the *Suns* came late this morning – after the boy had left."

"Then *you* must bring it."

"I will," I would assure her, "when the shop shuts at lunchtime."

"That is not good enough. You must bring it NOWWW!"

"Now?" Three people waiting for the post office - one with a huge parcel, the others flapping motor vehicle documents, two or three customers at the shop counter - one with a large basket of shopping.

" NOWWW!"

I put the phone down and took it off the hook. I served the customers, completed the morning, then slipped Mrs Shine's *Sun* through her letterbox. The next time I saw her she would have forgotten all about it.

CHAPTER FOUR.

PAPER TIGERS

I walk home across Knipplkes Bridge. It's eight o'clock, the day has hardly begun. I feel I've accomplished as much as if I had done a paper round. (**Peter Hoeg**: *Miss Smilla's Feeling for Snow.*)

The English teacher, the shopkeeper, the postmaster and the reserve paper boy set off to have a pint in the local pub. Not surprising really as they were all the same person. "Versatile" is a description that's often been applied to me. "Jack of all trades, master of none" is another but only by nasty, mean-minded people.

I enjoyed all my roles, even the role of paperboy. As the Peter Hoeg character above implies, there *is* a sense of accomplishment in doing a paper round. I always stood in when one of my regulars was unavailable and only on the mornings when I heard rain beating against the bedroom window did I feel any reluctance. Early mornings had their own magic, particularly on days when the sun was bathing the fields and the village was deserted. A paper round combined a sense of martyrdom with a sense of freedom, gave security and release in equal measure. And it was satisfying to know as I sat down to breakfast that a substantial part of the day's business had already been completed. On other mornings it was less enjoyable and as I watched the paperboys plunge off into the cold and wet, I would think of the passage from Bill Bryson's *Notes from a Small Island*:

> *Until 1847, children as young as four worked in the mines for up to ten hours a day and until...recent times boys of ten were put to work in total darkness in a small space.... from 3.a.m. to 4 p.m., six days a week.*

So there we have it. In darker times, a child's lot was unimaginable. Working in factories, sweeping chimneys, at the mercy of the wicked and the unscrupulous. All the spoilt kids of today have to put up with is paper rounds and the only wicked and unscrupulous character they encounter is the local shopkeeper.

I remember a television programme in which the "Long Johns", Bird and Fortune, were making fun of the Russian economy by drawing attention to the fact that everyone needed two jobs. The Minister of Defence doubled up as a taxi driver and if his phone rang on a Saturday night it could either be the President putting all nuclear defences on red alert or someone wanting a quick trip to the pizza parlour. My split occupations gave rise to similar anomalies and I can reasonably claim to be the only Third World educational consultant who doubled up as a paperboy. Once when giving a talk to a group of academics on some aspect of Sudanese Education, I reflected that earlier the same day I had been standing in the rain taking a verbal battering because Mrs Spiggot's bingo card wasn't in her *Daily Mail.* The fact that such occasions were rare was due to the reliability of the paperboys. In ten years we employed nine of them who varied from the reasonably good to the absolutely first-class.

BRITISH COUNCIL CONSULTANT AND
PAPERBOY

For much of the year, and notwithstanding my earlier remarks about bright summer mornings, a paper round is a sort of outward bound course with pay and should be a mandatory component of the Duke of Edinburgh's award. I've watched the boys cycle off in sub zero temperatures, in torrential rain, and in winds that would have daunted a lifeboat crew. Out into the bleak mornings they went with bags as big as themselves to contend with vicious dogs, alleys as dark as night, letterboxes hardly big enough for a post card, black ice on driveways, and villagers transformed into slavering monsters by a missing scratch card. One customer even complained that his paper was delivered later than someone else's as though by some sleight of hand all papers could be delivered at the same time. We witness the plight of refugees, hear of the dreadful rapes and murders of the innocent and in Poulton we complain about paper deliveries. In this case the complaint wasn't even about getting no paper or the wrong paper but getting the right paper in the wrong order! Are we pampered do you think? Or are we just...well, pampered?

To help a new paperboy, I marked up the papers. Some people commented that I didn't put the right names on them but fourteen-year-old boys have more important things on their minds than the name of the person who lives at the Old Farmhouse. I tried to relate the descriptions to the boys' own perceptions. Only one ever created any real amusement and that was a customer whose paper was put in a breadbin by the front door. I labelled the newspaper "Breadbin" and later found that the wife had taken it as a reference to her husband's stomach. Luckily, they had a sense of humour and afterwards, when phoning us with a query, would say "Bread-bin here" (some of the residents would have sued for less). Usually my descriptions weren't personal. I never put "Old Misery Guts" on any paper (on the grounds that it wouldn't have been exclusive enough). Then again, the Fuehrer, the Cheat, the Philistine, the Snob, the Stink Bomb, the Fusspot, the Crook, though perfectly intelligible to us, would have meant nothing to the paperboys.

As I said earlier, in ten years we employed nine paperboys and only one, the celebrated Jaffa Cake Kid, failed to survive the training period. The Jaffa Cake Kid had developed from a precocious child into a charming and highly intelligent adolescent. I had long earmarked him as a potential paperboy and he had shown some enthusiasm for the prospect so when a vacancy came up, I suggested to his mum that he might consider it. She expressed grave doubts on the usual grounds of his complete inability to get out of bed in the morning. I nodded, secretly poopooing such lack of faith. Hadn't I heard it from the mothers of all my paperboys? And hadn't they all seen their offspring transformed from Rip Van Winkles into veritable skylarks, getting up and out while the household was still asleep, returning to make pots of tea and chivvy younger siblings into catching the school bus; had seen them transformed from an early morning problem into an early morning solution. So I was sure the Jaffa Cake Kid would follow the trend and that his mother's doubts would be confounded.

   I was wrong. I had some reservations when he pitched up for his first training round and I hardly recognised him. It was as though he had spent all night buried alive and couldn't credit the fact that he'd been dug up. The body, the hair, the face were the same, yet this wasn't the Jaffa Cake Kid we knew and loved but some strange clone that had invaded his body. I waited confidently for him to change, waited for this sluggish caterpillar to become the lively young butterfly I saw every afternoon in the shop. I helped him, flattered him, cajoled him, even offered him a month's supply of Jaffa cakes but to no avail. He never threw off the cocoon of sleep. After three tortuous mornings, I accepted the inevitable an hour or so before it was confirmed. His mum came in with the news and smiled in an "I told you so" sort of way. I asked her what time the Kid made the transformation from member of the tribe of the walking dead to a sort of Einstein on skates. She couldn't put a time to it but thought that if I could arrange an evening delivery...

We commiserated and I looked elsewhere for my paperboy. The Jaffa Cake Kid, I'm sure, has a great future. He will do well at school, go on to university and be a roaring success in whatever field he chooses - as long as no early morning duties are involved. The Kid can be anything he wants to be. Except a paperboy.

"Put in a good word for me."
"With who?"
"The man in the shop."
"About what?"
"I want a paper round. I'm thirteen now. Put in a good word for me. Please?'

This conversation took place after we'd left the shop and I met the lad in question on his way home from school. Whenever he came into the shop I used to threaten to kick him out on the grounds that he was a football hooligan. Like all the customers I teased we had developed a good relationship and he now wanted me to give him a reference as a paperboy. What is this urge to do a paper round? I know I said earlier that a paper round is a great exercise in character building - and it is - but so is spending all night naked on the side of a snowswept mountain, lying for hours in a cold bath, spending a week at a party conference and no child has ever clamoured to do any of these things (except William Hague and he was a very strange child indeed). It's like someone rushing to the quay just as the last boat is leaving for a one-way trip up a crocodile-infested river and yelling in a panic-stricken voice "WAIT FOR ME!"

Anyway I promise I will put in a good word for him even though I don't know quite what word it'll be. I would hate him to miss out on such a life-enhancing opportunity.

So, parents, take note. A newspaper round changes a boy into a man. That snivelling adolescent you despaired of ever showing the remotest sign of growing up suddenly has a deeper voice, hairs on his chest and is bringing you cups of tea in bed. Get him a paper round as soon as possible. If there isn't a newsagent in the area, move to where there is one. And if the rounds are in short supply, get his name down early, even before he's born. People do this for Harrow and Eton and not even the best public schools can complete a child's education like a paper round. "Welcome to the real world" I felt like saying as I caught sight of a paper boy through the shop window, his face gaunt and frozen, his body wrapped from head to toe like Michelin man. "Welcome to the real world."

CHAPTER FIVE

CREDIT WHERE CREDIT'S DUE

I don't owe a penny to a single soul - not counting tradesmen of course! **(P.G. Wodehouse)**

We hadn't been in the business long before we realised that one way of boosting trade was to extend credit facilities. Harold had offered credit to a small number of customers. We increased the number substantially and encouraged anyone who regularly used the shop to open an account.

Giving credit had several advantages apart from boosting trade. Firstly, it gave customers a sense of belonging. They felt more welcome in an establishment where the owners invited them to help themselves to whatever they wanted and trusted them to settle up at the end of the month. Secondly, it removed one complication from the purchasing process, the need to have cash. A surprising number of people don't carry cash around with them and even if they do are reluctant to part with it. After opening an account, customers would buy more when they came to the shop and also pay us more visits.

Some shopkeepers are too calculating in their approach to credit, refusing to allow it on low profit items such as alcohol and cigarettes. This not only makes the system unnecessarily complicated; it is also likely to discourage customers from buying other items on credit. The last thing customers want is two separate arrangements for payment.

Offering credit also provided moments of amusement. The previous vicar and his wife were excellent customers, having a large order delivered every Friday and frequently calling at the shop on other days. On one occasion, the vicar helped himself to several bags of crisps and rode off with them in his saddlebag, completely forgetting that all purchases had to be recorded in the ledger. I phoned his wife who said in a tone of amused resignation "What's he been up to now?" I told her and expressed surprise that a man of the cloth could stoop to shoplifting. "They're the worst!" she replied.

Hand-in-hand with free credit facilities went our home delivery service. Order books were handed in during the week and the goods were delivered on Thursday or Friday when I had about a dozen deliveries to make. These involved delivering to what I came to think of as my "Friday night women" ending up at Frank Pitt's, one of the great local characters, where I was offered the largest whiskies I've ever encountered. When we sold the shop, delivering Frank's order was the one privilege I retained. Now I go and have my tipple without having to listen to complaints if the order's wrong or the tally is incorrect. "Don't blame me," I say sipping my drink, "I'm only the errand boy." Frank and his wife are long-standing supporters of the shop. Their dedication is unswerving and four generations of shopkeepers have delivered their orders.

To some customers, our delivery service was simply a variation on the old "Beer at Home" theme. No one took greater advantage of our "home brew" service than Lady Penn, a noted heroine of the Second World War.

Lady Penn's preferred tipple was vodka, a strange taste for such a quintessentially English lady - one would have imagined G and T with the occasional dry sherry. But vodka it was and there were many frantic phone calls from her housekeeper asking us to top up supplies that had become dangerously low - i.e. down to the last half dozen bottles. Lady Penn's experience in the French Resistance had rubbed off on her staff; the phone calls were cryptic and we alone knew that "V for victory" had nothing whatever to do with the war.

When we arrived in Poulton, Lady Penn was still active, driving round erratically in her old Rover 2000, with the registration letters "MAD". Later she became a recluse with all her orders made by phone. As I delivered them, I imagined a sort of Bates' Motel scenario with a crazy old woman, raddled with alcohol, lurking somewhere behind the oak door. On one occasion, however, I delivered in daylight and Lady Penn greeted me. In the years since I had last seen her, she hadn't changed at all; slim, graceful, impeccably dressed and well-spoken. Her reclusive life was obviously one of choice rather than necessity.

One Saturday morning the phone rang and Lady Penn's rather gruff aristocratic voice was on the other end asking me if I could deliver a dozen bottles of sherry as a matter of urgency.

"The thing is I've got some boys coming down from London for lunch and these lads are drinkers. Real drinkers," she added after a pause.

For someone who could have given Oliver Reed several drinks start and seen him under the table, this was an astonishing statement. I asked her what sherry she wanted - sweet or dry, expensive or cheap.

"Just give me the stuff you can't sell" she replied. "These boys aren't fussy. They'll drink anything."

I gathered together a dozen bottles of very dubious quality. I looked hard and long at the litre bottles of a British cream I had in stock but, drink anything or not, I decided I couldn't foist *those* on to an aristocratic household. In any case, Lady Penn had told me to give her the stuff I found difficult to sell and the litres of British cream were just about our *best* sellers for reasons that will become clear later.

But not even credit facilities and home deliveries could persuade the bulk of the village to shop with us on a regular basis though many used us in emergencies. One of the villagers we had never seen in the shop suddenly became a shopaholic, coming in every day and buying all her household requirements. She explained that her husband was in hospital and, as she didn't drive, she couldn't get to town. We sympathised and offered her credit, home deliveries and any other help she needed. She was very appreciative, and although we were sorry that her husband was ill, we were pleased that circumstances had conspired to introduce another person to the value of the shop and who we felt sure would be a permanent convert. It's an ill wind, as they say....

When her husband recovered, we never saw her again. She resumed her old shopping habits as though the period spent using the village shop had been an aberration. Which of course it had.

Whatever the reasons - insensitivity, thoughtlessness or just plain selfishness - she was certainly not appreciative enough to give us any more of her custom. Is it any wonder that village shopkeepers sometimes develop persecution complexes, the feeling of being misused by the community? We used to say to villagers who showed signs of abusing us: "We are here to be used, but not to be taken advantage of."

The distinction is important. We were happy to make special efforts on behalf of regular customers who asked for an item we didn't usually stock. In the same way, if we were short of anything for one of our home deliveries, we would get it from the nearby town, seeing it as part of our job to do everything possible to satisfy the requirements of people who supported us. On the other hand, the woman who expected us to store the frozen goods she had bought from the supermarket while she had coffee with a friend was taking us for granted. It was obviously an act of thoughtlessness and she was quite surprised when we refused. But surely when she'd had time to think about it, she would have understood our objection?

To revert to the main point, we offered credit to a wide variety of customers and were glad to do so. All the harbingers of doom who said we would be taken advantage of and that bad debts would multiply were wrong. As I point out several times in the course of this book, in twelve years we had only one bad debt, a resounding endorsement of both the honesty of our customers and the policy of giving credit.

CHAPTER SIX

FACTS AND FIGURES

Running a shop is often a lot of fun but also involves getting down to the brass tacks of business. And the brass tacks of business mean stock control, cash flow, customer relations and profit margins.

Profit from the business came from three categories: the post office salary which accounted for two fifths of the profit; newspapers which accounted for one fifth; and a category we referred to simply as "the shop" which accounted for the rest.

We assessed the return from each category in terms of time, space, capital and wastage. The post office involved a lot of time, little space, no capital and no wastage. The newspapers involved about an hour a day (albeit at an unsociable time), little space, little capital and little wastage. The shop involved a lot of time (shelf-filling, cleaning, cash-and-carry visits), a lot of space (virtually the whole of the shop area as well as storage above and at the back of the shop), almost all our working capital (we had at least £4000 tied up in stock at any one time), and, in these days of sell-by dates, substantial wastage.

Although we talk about the profit on a particular item, it is misleading to think that as you sell an item so you earn a percentage of its price. Profit has to be thought of as a percentage of capital outlay and no profit is made on the first items sold from a box. If the profit on an item is 20% and there are ten items in a box, the profit is only realised by the sale of the last two items so speed of turnover is an important factor in determining profitability. With this in mind, we divided the "shop" category into two - fast sellers and slow sellers. The fast sellers tended to be the ones favoured by passing trade - confectionery, cigarettes, crisps, canned drinks and, in the summer, ice cream. They had a high turnover and the capital invested quickly earned a profit. In addition they involved little space, little time and little wastage. They probably earned about half the "shop" income. Greeting cards were other items which, though not fast sellers, involved no wastage and little space or time. We put "sale or return" items into this category as well. A lot of our cards, the seeds, the locally grown flowers and the hosiery were sale or return items. Although they weren't necessarily fast sellers and the profit margins were understandably lower, they involved little work, no capital outlay, and absolutely no risk.

The other half of the shop income - canned foods, groceries, toiletries, washing powder, frozen food, pet food etc. took up most of the space, time, capital and wastage, turned over slowly, and realised a very modest profit.

We sometimes reasoned that if we got rid of everything but the post office, the newspapers and the fast sellers, we would save about two thirds of the shop space, eighty percent of storage and stock holding, and cut down our shelf-filling and cash and carry visits by around 75%. The idea was tempting but we rejected it. Had we rationalised in this way, the business would have been more efficient but would no longer have stocked the items that villagers needed and we could therefore no longer have claimed to be a proper village shop. We would have downsized to the detriment of our customers, in much the same way as bus companies did after privatisation - concentrating on the profitable routes and cutting out the rest. A large part of the service element in which we took such pride would have been eliminated.

But we *were* advised to rationalise in categories and not to offer too wide a choice in any one type of item. Chocolate bars are an example. Suppose a shop stocks only one type of chocolate bar and a box costs £10 with a profit margin of 20%. Most customers wanting chocolate and not finding their preferred choice will buy the one available. The box will be sold quickly and the profit realised. Now imagine that a shop stocks two types of bar and the same price and margin apply to both. Assuming both are equally popular, instead of selling one box and releasing the profit, you now sell two half boxes in the same period - perhaps a little more as you are now offering a choice - and haven't yet recovered your capital outlay, let alone made a profit. So the more capital spent on increasing choice, the slower the realisation of profit. Henry Ford reputedly told his customers "You can have any colour car providing it's black." A shopkeeper parodying this might say, "You can have any kind of chocolate bar providing it's a Mars." While no one would dream of going as far as this in an age when customers expect choice, it would be economic suicide to attempt to match supermarkets on selection. Even if you have the space to do so, there just isn't the market to generate the necessary speed of turnover.

We also had to rationalise in terms of the *amount* of any item we bought. Increasing numbers of products have sell-by dates and we couldn't afford to buy a twelve-item case of a slow-selling degradable product if we sold only one item every three months. Not only did it tie up capital, it also led to wastage. And as profit is only realised when the last items in a case are sold, on some bulk purchases we would often make a loss. This presented a problem when a regular customer requested such a product but we soon realised that the answer was to compromise and buy it singly from another shop. Although we made little profit on the item, the customer was satisfied and we didn't have a slow-moving (or no-moving) item on the shelves.

Another problem was that some suppliers operated a minimum order system. Their minimum was usually far more than we wanted to buy - an exception being ice cream in summer - and so we gradually disassociated ourselves from such suppliers. Managing a village shop, perhaps even more than managing other businesses, involves finding the right balance between cash flow and stock control and finding suppliers who allow orders according to your needs rather than to their regulations.

Just as we rationalised stock, so we rationalised layout. Harold had run a sharp little business but we felt that aspects of his layout could be improved. For example, his cleaning materials occupied a prominent place customers approaching the counter were confronted by the sight and smell of washing powder. This gave the shop the ambience of a laundrette and prevented a prime point of sale position being occupied by more enticing items. When we replaced the soap powder with fresh bread, chocolates and biscuits, many customers remarked how the atmosphere in the shop had improved.

The re-arrangement also increased sales. Because of its position - on a main road with good parking facilities - our shop attracted many customers looking for a snack, a drink, a newspaper or a smoke in the middle of a long journey. Ideally you want such customers to spend, say, a fiver each and you need items they are likely to buy sited in prime selling positions. As they're not local, they won't know the layout of the shop or what products you stock but it doesn't matter if some items aren't immediately obvious. Soap powder, tea, coffee, sugar etc. are all items for your regulars. If a passing customer can't see them, it's of little consequence but if he can't see the crisps or the chocolates you will lose sales. Soap powders are not impulse buys. No lorry driver waiting for a pie to be heated is likely to buy a packet of Daz. Crisps, chocolates, newspapers, cigarettes, yes. Ariel Automatic, no.

Another change we made was to take Tampax off the top shelf. Unless they happened to be of Amazonian height, women needing this potentially embarrassing item had to ask for assistance and the chances are, as in the old jokes about young men going into chemists for contraceptives, the more reticent among them would have emerged with a bottle of Lucozade and a packet of chewing gum. We decided that if we *had* to stock potentially embarrassing items, we should try to prevent customers being embarrassed by them.

What? People embarrassed by such things as Tampax in this free and easy age? Surely not. Well, let me tell you a story. Customers were always leaving things round the shop and on one occasion a tin of baked beans and sausages was left on the post office counter. All morning people drew my attention to this "tin of baked beans" in the tones of someone discovering a vital clue in a murder investigation. "And sausages, " a few added as though the sausages might explain why the tin was there in the first place.

People find it impossible to resist making the most banal observations. "Looks like somebody's broken one of your windows," someone would say seeing me on my knees sweeping broken glass from the floor; or "Did you know you had a leak?" on a day when water was pouring through the ceiling and Lizzie had just lent Joyce an umbrella. People will say almost anything rather than stand in silence. Every day, streams of meaningless utterances would penetrate the anti-bandit screen as I tried to concentrate on post office transactions. The customers who didn't talk blew air through their teeth in tuneless whistles. One even gave a passable impression of a trombone and punctured the silence with strange, hornlike sounds.

But to get back to the tin of beans. After lunch, a thought struck me and I replaced it with a packet of Tampax.

The post office was quite busy that afternoon. Customers were paying electricity bills and I issued quite a few vehicle licences. But no one drew attention to the object on the post office counter. Eyes drifted towards it, focussed, and drifted away. The silences grew, the tuneless whistles multiplied. Money, stamps, tax discs changed hands yet it was ten past five before anyone drew my attention to the packet of Tampax. Replacing a neutral object with an embarrassing one had turned the most garrulous of customers into Trappists.

One aspect of the business, which produced the occasional worry, was the fruit and vegetable trade. This increased substantially when Poulton's other shop closed and we acquired special shelving and created a well-stocked fruit and vegetable section that many customers relied on for last minute additions to their evening meals. Barbara and Kevin lived just down the road and Barbara was always popping in just before we closed. One day she burst in with "Sorry to come so late but I need a second vegetable." What could I say in response but "Isn't Kevin enough for you then?"

Occasionally we had a substantial amount of vegetables left and I would worry that the wastage was eating into our profits to the point where we might be making a loss. Lizzie and our wholesaler convinced me that such fears were groundless as the profit on fruit and veg - around 40% in many cases - was large enough to cater for the wastage involved. Goods retailing at £100, for example, would have cost us £60. This meant that even with wastage as high as 20% we would still be making 20% on sales. And not only is 20% an unusually high level of wastage, most of it wouldn't have been wastage at all as we would have used it ourselves.

The fruit and vegetable business proved a great boon. Not only was it profitable in itself, it also created a knock on effect and customers coming to buy fruit and vegetables would also buy other things. I heard a nice story the other day about a village shop that kept a minimal supply of fruit and vegetables. A customer came in and asked for a cauliflower. "We've sold it," the shopkeeper replied, "but we can order another for Friday." Apocryphal perhaps, but one that summarises the small shopkeeper's dilemma. We resolved it by erring on the side of the cauliflowers, deciding that a little wastage was preferable to dissatisfied customers. Occasionally it pays to use an accountant's logic to temper the emotional response produced by one or two mouldy vegetables. Not only were my fears unfounded, our prices for many items, even with a 40% per cent mark up, were still considerably lower than those of supermarkets. Mind you we did get rather tired of cauliflower cheese.

Prices were another area where a lot of hard thinking was involved. Just as we couldn't compete with the supermarkets on selection, neither could we compete with them on price and to have attempted to do either would have resulted in bankruptcy. Customers on the whole are remarkably ignorant of village shop economics. They will look at the price of an item and point out that it's 20p cheaper in Tesco, as if firstly we didn't know, and secondly we should lower our prices accordingly. We tried to complete their education by pointing out the following:

1. By buying in bulk, supermarkets often sell cheaper than village shops buy.

2. By *selling* in bulk, supermarkets can cut profit margins to the bone. For example, let's assume a supermarket and a village shop pay exactly the same price (£1) for an item. Over a period, the village shop sells ten of this item at £1.30. The supermarket sells 100 at £1.10 (20p cheaper) and still makes more than three times the profit.

3. The village shop is offering a different service from the supermarkets. The shop is there to serve the village - for impulse buys, for things the dependent villagers need and the others have left off their supermarket list. It relies on the fact that most shoppers are inefficient and that because they have forgotten to buy a jar of instant coffee at the supermarket, they will buy it locally, albeit at a higher price.

4. A trip to the supermarket involves travelling. Even discounting wear and tear on the car, the petrol alone for a ten-mile trip will cost over a pound and take the best part of an hour. For purchases up to £10, the village shop is cheaper and more convenient.

5. Not all supermarket products are either cheaper or better. Our free range eggs as well as our fruit and veg were much cheaper than Tesco's and several other items were comparable. However the price myth is now so well established that people find this difficult to believe. It always surprised us how well-disposed village residents were towards these superstores that exploit mercilessly, price other retailers out of business, leave town centres desolated and make fortunes for their directors and shareholders; and how correspondingly ill-disposed they are towards the little shop at the heart of their own community.

Buying a shop, as I said earlier, is a decision of the heart as well as the head and isn't in any sense based purely on profit. Had it been, we would never have bought one. The books we read before buying the business talked a lot about gross profit, net profit and real profit. Gross profit is the amount made from the act of buying and selling. Net profit is the gross profit minus overheads and all trading expenses such as electricity, wages, rates and so on. Real profit is the net profit minus the money you could have made as an employee and the interest that would have accrued on the capital tied up in the business. We thought of the shop as a one and a half person operation (I was the half!) and if we'd both taken outside jobs, even at a conservative estimate, we could have earned at least twice as much as the net profits from the business. In addition we had around £100,000 tied up in property and stock often at interest rates of around ten percent. So, even allowing for the fact that we weren't paying rent, it doesn't take a mathematician to work out that our real profit was actually a minus figure and that judged on purely economic criteria, committing ourselves to a post office stores was an act of folly. Yet we rarely felt this and there were obviously things other than the three kinds of profit to consider when justifying our choice of occupation.

In other words, the decision to buy a shop has to be based on things different to the normal criteria for buying a business. What we actually bought was not so much a business as a lifestyle. And whenever we rationalised our decision, this was the one element on which we placed a high premium. We had purchased a modest income but a high quality of life and this was why in spite of the occasional difficulties, we never had any serious regrets.

Another problem in running a shop is achieving a balance between too much and too little stock. This is particularly true when a product is a favourite purchase of one particular customer and often when we looked at the stock on our shelves, the presence of one item would remind us of someone no longer with us. Usually the item was liquor or tobacco.

Take for example Den and Rose Savey. Harold had come to an arrangement with Den and Rose, giving them credit to the value of one week's benefit payment and retaining their book as security. It was an arrangement that for the most part worked like a charm. Den was a pensioner with a face that had obviously worn out several bodies. Nobody knew how old he was - he could have been anything from 65 to a hundred. Rose was substantially younger - not yet fifty - and had been married before. Den was her second husband if Den was the improvement she claimed, we often speculated what her first must have been like.

Den and Rose lived in a remote cottage about three miles from Poulton. At the start, Rose did all their shopping on a ramshackle

old bike, pedalling off into the gloom with boxes tied to the handlebars and the rear mudguard. Later, they acquired an old banger, which was kept on the road by a mixture of luck and faith.

Monday was the day of Rose's "big shop" when a few items of food would be included among the hundred cheap cigarettes and several litres of a sweet sherry named after the royal household. Not that Den was either a patriot or a royalist but he was a drinker and always went for the cheapest sherry on the market. Litre after litre went off on the back of Rose's bike and we used to call the shop "Den's blood bank."

On Tuesday, Rose would do a "top up" shop with the bit of credit she had left - potatoes, bread, another two litres of sherry and another forty fags. Den was usually waiting in the car with his tongue hanging out and no doubt had a few swigs on the way home somehow managing to by-pass the drink-driving laws. No breathalyser could have coped with Den's breath. The surrounding air was probably over the limit.

Towards the end of the week, Rose would appear again, asking if "just this once" they could have a bit more credit. Invariably surprise visitors had dropped in; invariably these visitors lived exclusively on cream sherry and cheap fags. If the account was too far in the red, we would refuse. Den would then stoke himself up on whatever booze he had left and enter the shop like an avenging fury, cursing us to high heaven and threatening to withdraw his custom. He'd reclaim his benefit book and storm out vowing never to return. These fits of pique would last about a week after which Rose would reappear, hand back the book, and ask for sixty fags and two litres of sherry as though she'd never been away.

But eventually they did disappear, paying off their account and reclaiming their book. There had been no disagreement and we confidently expected them to return but they never did and we heard later that they'd moved to the nearby town and credit facilities anew. We were left with a case of sherry that we were hardly likely to sell to anyone else and a few months later we put it on special offer. We went away for the weekend and when we came back we were surprised to see that most of the sherry had gone. There is a species of moth that, during the mating season, can reputedly detect the female's scent at a distance of seven miles. Den obviously had the same capacity for sniffing out special offers on sherry and, like Dracula rising from the grave, had made one last appearance at his blood bank.

When another couple moved away, the packets of Silk Cut 100's and Dunhill International, items which previously had the shortest shelf life of all, now languished for months, a reminder that Major Otter and his wife no longer lived in the village. The major was an army man through and through, wearing his blues on every occasion and immaculate in everything apart from his language which was liberally sprinkled with the "F" word irrespective of time, location or company. After a few years in the village, he became co-ordinator of the Neighbourhood Watch Committee, a role he performed with boundless enthusiasm. On taking over, he sent out a circular saying it was "incumbent on villagers to be vigilant and aware of their surroundings". The circular ended with an invitation to attend a Neighbourhood Watch meeting the following Friday in the village hall. "By the way," he said when he brought the circulars into the shop for us to distribute, "Where *is* the village hall?"

His wife was the self-styled Poulton witch and after the post office robbery (described later) she became very concerned about our well-being. Before one Neighbourhood Watch meeting she said that there was no need for *me* to worry about crime as she had placed a protective ring round the post office. Her husband overhearing this exclaimed, "Why not place a protective ring round the whole village. Save us all this f...ing trouble."

Another Major sadly made a more permanent departure. He and his wife lived in a neighbouring village and started using the shop a short time after we took over. He was a sweet man with an incurable illness, a battle-axe for a wife and a craving for the only vice left to him - nicotine. They opened an account and the woman scrutinised it regularly to make sure he wasn't buying cigarettes. Eventually we started putting his cigarettes down as cabbages, apples, fruit juice, all the healthy options. She wasn't fooled. After all, when did a cabbage cost £2.85? Even at village shop prices.

Beneath the gruff exterior, she was surprisingly good-natured and when he died she was heartbroken. They crossed our lives for a few years, then disappeared, he into the oblivion of eternity, she into immobility and old age. She lent me a book of Mary Wilson's poems in 1992 with the instructions to return it within a week. We're now into the new millennium. I really must give it back. But the packets of Embassy Mild were a sad relic of her husband's departure. As the litres of dry cider, the Clan tobacco, the one or two bottles of Hock were equally poignant reminders that Mr. Barnett, Mr. Winner and Mrs. Bird were also no longer with us. That for a long time they still had places on the shelves of their local shop underlined in a strange way what the shop meant, or should have meant, to the village. Their favourite purchases were a kind of non-musical requiem.

CHAPTER 8.

DEALING WITH THE PUBLIC.

The public is two distinct things - a great homogenous mass with similar preoccupations - family, the weather, jobs, money, food - and a collection of individuals each capable of behaving completely unpredictably and whose antics we found endlessly fascinating.

One of our more independently-minded customers, when hauled before the magistrates on a drink-driving charge, rejected the authority of the courts to pass judgement on him and used his case to challenge the validity of the entire English legal system. One had to admire his principles if not his sense. When anyone questioned the wisdom of what he was doing, he would often go off in a huff which, as someone remarked, was one of the few modes of transport he had left! After further brushes with the law and some interesting instances of defending himself at the appeal court, he was given a spell of community service. He refused to perform this and went "on the run" to escape the custodial fate that awaited him. He would, however, make the occasional appearance in the village shop. On one of these sorties, just as he was deciding which of the freezer meals he would purchase for his supper, he felt a hand on his shoulder and heard a voice say: "I don't think you'll be wanting frozen food where *you're* going." The episode was straight out of *Dixon of Dock Green*.

Customers come in different shapes and sizes. There are the customers who are briskly efficient and expect to come in, get their shopping, pay and be out again without breaking stride. At the other end of the scale are those who seem to have all the time in the world.

"I'm sure I've got the exact change" one of them would say, delving into the depths of his pocket and producing an assortment of peppermints, paper clips, buttons, bits of string, a boiled sweet or two all loosely bound together by a strange substance that I shall dignify with the name fluff. I wait as he disentangles three pence from this odd assortment. "Don't want to break into another 10p now do we?" All this time I've been hovering over the till like a concert pianist waiting for the conductor to give the word. When he finally comes up with the exact money, he drops half of it on the floor and listens as it rolls in sundry directions, at least one coin ending up under the freezer. "Looks like you'll have to crack that 10p after all," I say, watching in dismay as he sinks to his knees and starts scrabbling frantically around.

"Won't keep you a minute," I assure the next customer as I strive to move the freezer. By this time, there's a long queue, the dog's barking and the phone's ringing. "Got it!" he says triumphantly, holding up a coin that looks like a relic from the pre-decimal age. In fact it *is* a relic from the pre-decimal age. "I'll come back when you lot have joined the twentieth century," one impatient individual says slamming the door behind him.

To other customers, the request for payment seems to come as a complete surprise. You total up their shopping and ask them for £5.80 or whatever and only then do they realise money is required and delve into their handbags for their purses. A few seconds later (it seems an age) the purse emerges and the agonising process of counting out the exact money begins. It invariably ends a few pence short so another compartment is opened and you half expect a few moths and spiders to emerge with the ten pound note. Paint couldn't dry more slowly.

There are also what I called the dribs and drabs customers. They put a couple of things on the counter and when you've entered them on the till (but never before) decide there's something else they need and disappear to the back of the shop while you wait, the till clogged, the whole operation of the shop at a standstill while they find whatever it is they've forgotten. And some customers do this three or four times. Then, just before the end of a quiet day, you decide to start the tidying up process early. You've just finished cleaning and disinfecting the ham slicer when, hey presto, the door opens and in comes a customer. You know before she opens her mouth what she's come in for. One *thin* slice of ham. You're certain she doesn't actually want the ham but is buying it purely out of spite. Otherwise how could such a thing happen so regularly?

Then there are the "helpful" customers, the ones who, when you're halfway through counting their change, say "I can give you 21p if it's any help." This throws your mental processes into total confusion and you have to start again.

Queues are another fascinating study. A place in a queue is part of an English person's birthright and queue jumpers are viewed with the odium usually reserved for child molesters. People will often give up their place in the queue to someone whose business will be quicker than theirs but react with ill-concealed venom should anyone take it without their consent. Watching the life-threatening scramble for buses and cinema seats that takes place in countries which have no concept of queuing, one can only be grateful for the English person's sense of order even if it occasionally leads to bouts of unbelievable pusillanimity.

Some customers never stopped talking and seemed to think that one of the duties of the village shopkeeper, was to listen to the most trivial details of the life history of some distant relative. Many of them could, as the saying goes, bore for England. An innocent comment on the weather would lead to a detailed history of their family's special occasions and how the weather had made or marred them. "My second cousin's wedding – lovely girl looked a bit like Julie Christie – completely destroyed by the rain. The bridesmaid's bouquets were totally ruined. Took place in a little church in the West riding just on the edge of the Moors. Mind you, I didn't hold with it. He was a Norwegian and I'm not at all sure that..." All this from an unguarded remark of mine that it "looks a bit like rain." At such times I would glaze over and hope I was nodding and shaking my head at the right moments. With some customers I learned to say nothing, not even "Hello". Some were veritable time bombs of verbosity who needed no fuse to get them going. Even "Hello" was seen as an invitation to recite chapter eight hundred and sixty three of their personal history, so I tried to stay silent. One was so self-absorbed you could disappear for a few minutes and return to find her cheerfully engaged in the same dreary monologue.

Other customers made a habit of never bringing enough money to the shop. They would walk in, spend seventy-eight pence and then find they'd only got a 50p piece. And it happened with monotonous regularity. The till was permanently littered with scraps of paper saying things like "Miss Peabody owes 32p." I used to wonder what they had against carrying a bit more money with them. Poulton is hardly the mugging capital of the world. "Live dangerously," I felt like saying. "Next time you come, put a pound coin in your pocket."

One woman spent half an hour examining various products for E-numbers and other additives and having satisfied herself that all the products she was buying were completely free of unhealthy additives, asked for twenty fags and a bottle of whisky. Oh the vagaries and idiosyncrasies of human nature revealed in the daily operations of a village shop!

But the beauty of running a village shop is that frustration, humour and pathos are nicely balanced in customer relations and experiences. One of the saddest things about living in a community that consists mainly of older people is that over a comparatively short period many of them die and one of our least pleasant duties was attending the funerals that occurred with sad regularity. But most were convinced they were going to a better place and they left us with many happy and amusing memories.

Like old Joe Cook who, just after we took over the shop, started having a cup of tea with us. Initially he accepted this hospitality with much appreciation and humility but gradually things changed. I don't remember precisely when the privilege became a right; I do know that instead of me greeting him with "Would you like a cup of tea?" he was greeting me with "Put the kettle on, then." And so, just after three every day of the week, vehicles remained unlicensed, pensions uncashed, letters unstamped, bills unpaid - all activity suspended while I boiled the kettle and poured hot water over two teabags. I poured a cup for myself as well but by this time the shop was so full that I rarely had time to drink it. Meanwhile Joe sipped and gloated, perched contentedly on the chair specially provided for the purpose.

TEA TIME

Not only did *Joe* come to expect his tea, other people came to expect it for him.   People I barely knew would come in and ask, "Has he had his tea yet?" And woe betide me if the answer was no. However urgent their business, there was a general consensus that Joe's tea had a kind of divine precedence and they waited patiently until the cup was safely in his hand. I should add, in the spirit of accuracy rather than criticism, that the gesture was never recipro-cated. Many a morning as I struggled against the elements in the course of a paper round, Joe would taunt me from the warmth of his living room, raising a steaming mug to the window and grin-ning devilishly.

Joe became something of a talisman and if he missed a day, a hole appeared in our lives. Like the apes and Gibraltar, we felt that if he stopped coming, the whole enterprise might, metaphorically, fall into the sea.

The relationship was by no means one-sided. Joe used the shop for much of his family's shopping and also helped us to unpack stock and deliver the local papers. He enjoyed the teasing and the insults that I threw at him and if I was polite (which I rarely was) he thought he'd upset me and his wife would urge me to start insulting him again.

Some people regarded Joe as an extra burden on our already burdened lives. One customer actually said that we must find "the cheek of that old man a bit hard to take", as though Joe was an intruder who by some mysterious means managed to extort daily cups of tea out of us. Comments like that made us despair. There was this benign, humorous, weather-beaten old man who had become something of a tourist attraction, and at least one customer thought we should tell him where to get off. We resented Joe so much that we provided him with a chair, a walking stick, and a bench outside to use in warm weather. I used to tease him that his wife deserved the George Cross for surviving fifty years of marriage, that he spent so much time in the shop the Council were trying to charge an extra poll tax, and that he'd been there so long he was in short trousers when he first came in. He was very fond of my daughter and once said he would like to marry her. The idea of Joe as my son-in-law brought the house down.

But the day arrived when Joe couldn't come anymore. His legs had deteriorated to the point where he could hardly walk and although I collected him a few times in the car, his confidence had gone and with it the old sparkle. A short time later his wife died and a year later Joe died too. But the shop survived the death of a customer we thought vital to its well-being. Joe went, and later we also left and the shop is, thankfully, still carrying on. No matter how much we sometimes flatter ourselves to the contrary, no one is indispensable.

Joe in fact provided our first lesson on the social importance of the shop. Village shops may *need* the rest of the village but they are *about* the Joe Cooks. The shop was a pivotal aspect of his life. It was the reason for his daily walk, provided many of his family's household needs, enabled him to cash his pension and pay his bills and gave him regular contact with people. It was part of his life support system and without it his quality of life would have been inestimably poorer.

Miss Cocker, the evil-smelling woman referred to in a previous chapter, was one of those who kept a maternal eye on Joe and his tea. Knowing my assumed aversion to making it, she would pop in while he was there, fix me with an accusing eye and inquire sternly "Has he had his tea yet?" In fact, once we had come to terms with her smell, we realised that Miss Cocker was an engaging personality with a mind as sharp as a needle and a wicked sense of humour. An ongoing joke in the shop was our dislike of supermarkets and Miss Cocker would sprinkle her conversation with emphatic eulogies to "Tesco" and "Waitrose."

But there was yet another side to Miss Cocker - generosity and compassion. When she found out about my trips to Khartoum, the week before I left she would give me twenty pounds from her pension saying "Give it to the people who really need it."

So in Khartoum I would find a currency dealer and change Miss Cocker's money. The rate was increasingly favourable as the Sudanese currency was in a state of ongoing collapse and I was able to hand out bundles of Sudanese notes to the children living rough in the streets. There was a nice symmetry in the children from the city of a thousand smells being given succour by Miss Cocker. It didn't change their long-term situation but for two or three days those children didn't need to worry where the next food was coming from. Thanks to the kindly old woman from a different culture and a village thousands of miles away, for a little while they felt like kings.

Few people knew this side of Miss Cocker and I was pleased that at her funeral, Peter Jeffries, the local vicar, whose obituaries were always so complete and personal, made a reference to it. As she was buried, I recalled the lines from *Oklahoma:* "The daisies in the dell will give out a different smell, because poor Judd is underneath the ground." I haven't noticed any change in the perfume of the flowers in Poulton churchyard. What I do know is that, when she died, Poulton lost one of its great characters. The air may be purer but the village is the poorer for the absence of this quick-witted, generous old lady.

Miss Cocker was lucky that despite her age – she was well into her eighties – she had retained all her mental sharpness. Many of our other customers were fiercely independent old people whose faculties had diminished. They drove round the countryside with fading eyesight and defective memories in cars that should have been scrapped years before. Yet given the skeletal nature of the local bus services, cars were the only way they could get around and they kept them on the road in the face of all mechanical and optical logic. There were several minor accidents outside the shop. Once we thought a ferocious assault had been made on the fence guarding the war memorial on the other side of the road but it had simply been an old lady mistaking the accelerator for the brake.

There were other stories, some amusing, others less so. One day, I drove home, parked the car, and forgot to put the handbrake on. The car rolled backwards, careered across the road and demolished a neighbour's wall. The neighbours were very understanding and told us about a woman who had done the same thing. She had gone into the post office and as the car rolled forward, a dog sitting in the back leapt into the driver's seat. Looking out of their window, they saw the car trundling down the road with the dog standing on its hind legs, its paws on the steering wheel.

Another "car" story relates to Poulton's eccentric millionaire, G. J. G. J. was an essentially lonely man. I never saw him without reflecting that the only thing money guarantees is the chance to be miserable in comfort. Beneath a cool veneer, he had a kind heart, often playing the Lord Bountiful role and buying boxes of Kit-Kat, pallets of tomato soup, and trays of Coca Cola to give his workers. He had a habit of cruising round in his Bentley and parking it outside the post office while he went for a stroll round the village.

Six months or so after our arrival in Poulton we invited two old friends to supper. Although John and Liz lived close by, we hadn't seen them for years and as they drove into Poulton the first thing they saw was this gleaming green monster parked outside our house. John's first response was "Bloody hell, fancy Stuart having a car like that." The thing that shocked him was not that I had the money to *buy* a Bentley, but that I'd actually *bought* one. He didn't think I was the type. We reassured him by showing him *our* car, a five-year-old Escort Estate with signs of rust on its bodywork, a car much more indicative of both our personalities and our finances.

We realised early in our tenure the embarrassment - to ourselves and our customers - which could result from an unguarded remark. Although this is true in any walk of life, the possibilities are greater in a village shop where much social intercourse occurs and where tongues tend to be looser. There was the occasion, for instance, when a young woman changed the address on a man's pension book and Lizzie said how nice it would be to have her father living with her. "He's not my father. He's my husband!" the woman replied.

Another woman said to Lizzie. "Tommy's not at all well. I'm very worried about him."

The next time she saw the woman Lizzie asked if her husband was better to which the woman retorted "Tommy isn't my husband. He's my dog."

In spite of a few further faux pas, we gradually learned the lesson. In a small, closely-knit community, it's important to find out who people are and how they are related to others before risking well-meaning comments. Village shop proprietors are no more immune than the rest of the population from opening their mouths and putting both feet in.

So diplomacy was called for in many of our dealings. One woman was convinced that an elderly neighbour had a long-standing grudge against her and every night about 2 a.m. would make an assault on the world high jump record by vaulting the eight foot hedge surrounding her property and commit mayhem in the rose bushes. We somehow had to sympathise and at the same time avoid giving credence to what was obviously a bad case of paranoia. It wasn't easy. Then there were the two neighbours who supported us, shopped regularly with us but couldn't stand the sight of each other. We heard detailed accounts of each set of grievances and gave our undivided loyalty to whichever one we happened to be listening to while praying that we would never be called to mediate.

There was also the time when another elderly lady had taken something of a shine to a young local builder. One day, he was checking our wood burning stove and she saw his van parked outside. She asked if I'd seen him and just as I was about to say that he was in our living-room, Lizzie appeared and hastily forestalled me. "We haven't seen him for weeks," she said airily. The woman looked puzzled.

"But his van's outside."

"His brother's borrowed it," said Lizzie, adlibbing admirably and the woman reluctantly left. I went into the lounge and found the builder hiding behind the settee.

No moment had greater potential for embarrassment, however, than the day we heard a man and a woman discussing a wedding The conversation went something like this.

Woman: "I saw you at the Keating wedding on Saturday."

Man:　"Did you?"

Woman (nodding): "Wasn't it ghastly?"

The man muttered incoherently and left. The woman, looking slightly puzzled, shrugged and carried on with her business. She didn't know - and we chose not to tell her - that the man she had been speaking to was the person responsible for the "ghastly" wedding, the father of the bride.

CHAPTER EIGHT

PERSONAL SERVICE

"So what's it going to do today," a customer asked as he paid for his newspaper. I glanced through the window at the dark clouds skudding overhead.

"Rain this morning, brightening up later."

"I'll hold you to that," he said as he went out, almost bumping into a woman who had pulled up outside.

"Couple of sheep loose on the Fairford Road," she said popping her head through the doorway. "Thought you ought to know."

I nodded and got on the phone to the only sheep farmer I knew in that area. I'd just finished when one of our regulars rushed in.

"Can you help me," she said almost in tears. "I've locked myself out and left a cake in the oven. I'm afraid it'll burn the house down."

Calling on Lizzie to take over, I grabbed a hammer and my burglar's mask. Five minutes later I had effected a successful break-in and earned her undying gratitude. In less than half-on-hour, the roles of meteorologist, shepherd and housebreaker had been added seamlessly to our range of (unpaid) services.

Running a village shop involves a rare combination of skills and personal characteristics. Few things must be beyond you, absolutely nothing beneath you. Once, as I thought about our lives as shopkeepers, lines from Dryden drifted back about a character who

> In the course of one revolving moon
> Was chemist, fiddler, statesman - and buffoon.

The sentiments are apt. To run a village shop you need to be an accomplished (if hammy) actor, a counsellor, a humorist, a book-keeper, with the strength of Hercules and the patience of Job. You need an encyclopedic memory for the hundred and fifty post office transactions plus a felicity for looking up the hundred and forty that you invariably forget. Add the accuracy of a draftsman, the forecasting ability of Cassandra, the mental agility of a grasshopper to switch from dealing with an overseas parcel one minute to working out the price of cheese the next and you can see this is no job for ordinary people.

The personality of the owner plays a disproportionately large part in the success of a village shop. Customers use the shop for a variety of reasons - because it's convenient, because they want it to survive, and so on. But whatever their motives, the shop has to be a pleasant place to visit. In addition, with such a small market base, the shop can afford no suggestion of exclusivity. The three hundred or so residents of Poulton cover a range of socio-economic groupings and the shop needs customers from all of them. We tried to treat everyone as equals and felt that the local Lord was no more entitled to special privileges than our less well-heeled customers. Our aim was to turn the shop into "a classless society" (to borrow John Major's phrase) and we like to think we achieved it.

In providing personal service, the village shop has a major advantage over supermarkets. All right, so supermarkets offer a far greater range of goods at slightly cheaper prices but try going to Tesco's if you want a pint of milk and haven't any money, or if your husband's run off with the girl from the stables and you want a shoulder to cry on. Try asking the checkout girls to direct you to Mrs. Jones of Fairview or Joe Bloggs of Willow Farm and witness the blank looks or the frank irritation. Try asking them for change when you desperately need the phone, or the loo when you're in the middle of a long journey and your youngest child is on the verge of fouling the seat of your brand new Peugeot. And how often have supermarkets found homes for old people, or attracted people back because the atmosphere is relaxed and amusing, or encouraged people who haven't seen each other for weeks to stand and gossip while trade goes on around them? Whether we like it or not - and usually we do - people expect us to be there (until we're not) and to have a range of knowledge way beyond our social status. In the course of an hour you may have to decide whether a man can tax his car (the tax ran out the month before last), work out the latest price of tomatoes, direct somebody to the local psychiatrist (you often feel like following them), cancel someone else's papers as they're off for a month's pony-trekking in the Andes (you don't envy them of course - can't ride a pony and don't like heights), take the order for the week's eggs, and decide whether you can afford to buy three varieties of cheese this week. Then out of the corner of your eye you see someone brandishing a cheque-book and drop everything to tot up his bill (not that this would ever take priority over the man who only wants directions). One day, my first "customer" was a water board official wanting to know where not one but *six* houses were located. I told him, and as a parting shot asked him in his own interest to pray for the survival of village shops.

Customers expect village shopkeepers to recognise them and treat them as individuals. They're not simply cash going into the till (well they are but we have to pretend they're not), but human beings with their own problems and personalities and we tried to make them feel special in a variety of ways. Firstly, we tried to stock items they particularly wanted, going out of our way to make sure we had their favourite brands of tobacco, whisky or breakfast cereal. We also assigned to many of them a slight idiosyncrasy, a way of singling them out for personal treatment. This was part of the social aspect of the shop, what one customer described as the pastoral dimension we brought to the work. We tried to amuse them, cheer them up, and bring something different into their lives by giving them a kind of social monogram.

At least this is what we hoped we were doing.

There was Mr Mills from across the way. He and his wife were comparative newcomers to the village and they used us for the post office, bread and the occasional bottle of red wine. On one occasion, I said to a customer, "You've heard of England's "dark satanic mills". Well, he's right behind you." Mr Mills took it all in great good humour. From then on he became "Dark Satanic", which was shortened to D.S. His wife became Mrs D.S. These personal touches - based on sympathy or humour - were part of the job of maintaining good customer relationships and creating a convivial atmosphere which would make people want to visit the shop again.

There was a woman from a nearby village who came in once or twice a week for her magazines and odd bits of shopping. I always called her the first thing that came into my head - Gladys, Gertrude, Henrietta - *anything* but her real name. She responded by calling me Clarence or Humphrey. I once had a spin on her tandem when Lizzie and I were planning our version of "A Bicycle made for Two" in the Poulton Music Hall. The experience was exhilarating - at least for me. "Gertrude" I think found it a little unnerving."Henrietta" works as a receptionist at the local surgery. The last time I saw her there I handed her a urine sample unable to resist the comment: "Now it's you who's taking the piss."

There were many similar examples. One customer we mistakenly called Milly (perhaps because she liked to think of herself as thoroughly modern). We'd been calling her Milly for over a year when she coyly informed us that her name was actually Joan. "But please carry on calling me Milly," she added. "I rather like my new name!"

I teased one woman who made a habit of coming in around 5.25. Later she changed her routine but whatever time she came in, I would look at my watch, pretend it was 5.30 and comment on how the day had flown. Another customer was Mrs. Milk who always used to buy milk (and other things) from us. Later she dropped the milk and only bought the other things but still retained the name Mrs. Milk. Another girl once had to wait quite a time before being served. The next time she came in I remarked, "Shan't keep you more than half an hour." Quick as a flash she replied "Oh, you're moving quickly today then."

This approach to customers started unobtrusively, but after a few years it had become an essential aspect of our customer relations and we liked to think that the other customers enjoyed the banter that went on around them. Occasionally one would twitch a little thinking he was being kept waiting. If he had looked more closely he would have seen that I served as I talked - unlike ex-President Ford, and in spite of what Lizzie says, I *can* walk and chew gum at the same time - and that nothing was added to his waiting time while I exchanged a few pleasantries with the customer in front. Or he could have remembered that he was in a village shop where speed is not the only criterion.

Of course it's not only pleasantries and jokes that are exchanged but scandal and gossip, those intimate little bits of information that are usually whispered behind closed doors. As one of Congreve's characters remarked:" I know it's a secret for it's whispered everywhere." "Particularly in the village shop," he could have added.

Our dealings with customers were generally interesting and entertaining but running a village shop also involves a few of the most tedious activities ever devised by man.   One afternoon, a chap asked me about our impending retirement. I was re-stocking the baked beans at the time (not, I imagine, one of my parents' great ambitions for me as I gurgled in my cot).

"You won't know what to do with yourself," he retorted as three baked beans tins toppled on to my foot and I yelped in pain.

"You'll be bored to tears!" How ridiculous, we thought. Surely people have far too many interests in retirement to dream of being bored. Then a few days ago we were reading the *SAGA Magazine* (yes we receive such publications now) and came across a letter which began "I really must write and put the other side of the argument concerning the public toilets in Melton Mowbray." So you see there are all kinds of unresolved issues out there to help retired people stave off boredom.

CHAPTER NINE.

THE AGE OF INNOCENCE

Easter in Pembrokeshire. We were spring-cleaning our holiday chalet and BBC radio was taking a trip down memory lane to the days when the nine o'clock slot on Saturday morning was filled by *Children's Favourites* and presented by a character called Uncle Mac who played the children's requests - Max Bygraves singing about the pink and blue toothbrushes, Burl Ives wallowing in the *Big Rock Candy Mountain*, and those classic Danny Kaye emoters - *The Ugly Duckling, Inchworm, Thumbelina*, and many many more. We were taken back to the days when children were children, when sex, smoking, and alcohol were for adults, and drugs for nobody at all.

Then, halfway through painting the bathroom, we heard a harsh chord on an electric guitar. Elvis and *Heartbreak Hotel* had arrived, and the days of innocence had gone forever.

Except in the village shop.

The village shop is the last retail establishment where children can go and exercise a modicum of independence. Children hardly ever go to supermarkets without an adult in attendance but they were always popping into our shop on an errand for their parents or to spend their pocket money. The shop gave them their first experience of economics - deciding that they wanted something and working out whether they could afford it. We occasionally let them off a few pence if their money didn't quite match the prices on the shelves. (Prices, after all, are arbitrary. They are not some universal truth sent down from the mountain with Moses but frequently decided on the basis of whether we had a plastic five or a plastic six to put on the shelf edging.)

We were pleased when children used the shop and also when they took advantage of the basic financial training offered by the Post Office by opening National Savings accounts. Encouraging children to save was one of the traditional functions of the post office. They would fill out deposit slips in spidery writing and hand over their pocket money or the contents of their money boxes which often amounted to something like £3.78. Counting it was a chore we were happy to undertake. A National Savings account gave the children a sense of control, the feeling that they were doing something, however small, to influence their lives. It was a mechanism for them to save up for something they wanted - carriers for their bikes, Christmas presents, the latest pop CDs, junk food beanos - it didn't matter. They were being trained in saving and budgeting and given a taste of independence. Then the Post Office, in its cost-cutting wisdom, introduced a minimum deposit of £10 and the financial training ended.

Just after this regulation had been introduced, I told a customer that the two pounds his son wanted to deposit was now unacceptable.

"God, what's happening to this place?" he complained as if it was my fault. "Where's the training gone?"

"Don't blame me," I said. "I'm on your side." He clearly didn't believe me and obviously had no idea of our inability to deflect, let alone reason with or control, the bureaucratic juggernaut known as the Post Office.

But in spite of the killjoy antics of our bureaucratic Scrooge, the village shop is still one of the last bastions of childhood and the kindly shopkeeper a character straight out of Enid Blyton. Poulton no longer has a school but in villages that do, the shops do a roaring trade as "tuck shops". The grandson of the local lord always bought about £10 worth of "tuck" the day before he was whisked away to boarding school to start another term. It is unwise for any shopkeeper to alienate the "tiny trade" as, though the amounts children spend individually may be small, collectively they add up to a sizeable part of the week's business. In addition, children have parents who are often influential in forming village opinion and stories of Dickensian shopkeepers will spread like wildfire. If this makes us sound like calculating Zvengalis, using children for what we might get out of them, it's not true (well, not completely). Humane attitudes are not *always* incompatible with good business practice. In addition, it was a privilege to welcome (well-behaved) children into the shop and we gained a great deal of amusement from them. The Jaffa Cake Kid is mentioned elsewhere. Some of our other favourites were Ginger Beer, (Jemima) Puddleduck, the Monster, the Liverpool Supporter and Rhydian, the Welsh boy who didn't recognise a leek. There were Toby and Rachel and our teasing attempts to create a childhood romance. "I don't like her," Toby exploded one day. "I don't even *love* her!"

Last but not least there were "the terrible twins" who had our nerves on edge every time they came into the shop. Their mother was a delightful, eccentric, disorganised woman whose heart was in the right place - even if her children frequently weren't, She would completely ignore them as tore round the shop interfering with displays, taking items from shelves and screaming blue murder till they got the ice cream they wanted. They would turn cartwheels with bottles of vinegar in both hands, while their mother talked about the morality of road building and the eccentricities of the farming lobby. It was like conducting a Socratic debate in a crowd of football hooligans.

She once asked Lizzie whether her children were the worst behaved in the village. I would have said: "Why restrict it to the village?" Lizzie simply said, "Yes." From that day the children behaved better and the mother never took offence. I said to her one day as they came into the shop "How are the children from hell?" She replied: " Back where they belong!"

A lovely woman. Pity there's not more like her.

And although other children sometimes misbehaved and occasionally tried our patience, we would never have gone to the extent of banning them as one other local business did. It was part of our job to accommodate them as they thrust their way into the shop scouring the chocolate display with eager eyes before emptying their pennies on the counter. *Heartbreak Hotel* may have heralded the era of teenage crime and childhood pregnancies but we came down heavily on the side of the *Big Rock Candy Mountain*. As Peter Sellars once remarked: "You may not realise it, sir, but some of our greatest men and women started life as children."

CHAPTER TEN

AWAY FROM IT ALL.

"How often do you manage it?" a psychiatrist in *Fawlty Towers* asked Basil.

"Three or four times a week if you must know," Basil blurted out, convinced they were talking about sex.

They were in fact talking about holidays.

"Not once in fifteen years," would have been the response of at least one pair of shopkeepers we came into contact with. "Once or twice a year," would have been our reply, "but only by courtesy of Joyce."

Arranging holidays is a major headache for subpostmasters. They have to find somebody reliable to run the shop and the post office and be able to afford them. The Post Office doesn't make it easy for breaks to be arranged particularly with regard to cancelling the balance and claiming the substitution allowance.

A postmaster is responsible for his office fifty two weeks a year and apart from Sundays and public holidays, post offices are required to open every day. A postmaster is officially entitled to seven weeks substitution allowance every two years at a specified daily rate. I often called the substitution allowance holiday pay but this was misleading. In other jobs you take a holiday and you get paid for it. That is holiday pay. As a subpostmaster, you arrange a holiday, then you find someone to take over your office during your absence. The money that you claim from the Post Office to pay this person is the "substitution allowance."

There is an important difference between the two terms. Paid holidays are accepted as a right by almost all workers and employers. An employee arranges his holiday at a particular time, informs his employer who arranges for his work to be covered by one or more of his colleagues, and off he goes camping, pony-trekking, sunbathing or lager-louting to his heart's content. This applies to permanent staff and most workers in all businesses including, I should add, the Post Office.

Except subpostmasters. When a subpostmaster goes on holiday, he must ensure that the holiday doesn't coincide with the end of a month, apply for permission to be away from his office, find at least one but preferably two people who are capable of running the business in his absence, give their names to the Post Office and ensure they are clued in to all possible eventualities. He will do this knowing that the remuneration he will get from the Post Office to cover these substitutions will be inadequate and subject to several conditions. The substitute must not be a member of the postmaster's family and anyone who usually works in the Post Office must only claim over and above their normal wages. The allowance is then applied for *in retrospect*. When we first took over, these rules were very loosely applied but application has now become tighter and we even heard of one subpostmaster losing his job through "fraudulent substitution claims", that is when his substitute was a member of his family.

I have suggested to several Post Office representatives that the fairest system would be to include the substitution allowance in the postmaster's salary and let him decide whether to use it for holiday purposes or not. It would cut out yet another bureaucratic procedure, and prevent people compromising their honesty by lying about something they believe to be their right. Probably *because* it's the most sensible option, it stands little chance of being implemented.

The balance was the other hurdle that had to be overcome before we could get away. About halfway through our tenure, the Post Office changed balance night from Friday to Wednesday, a welcome adjustment as the weekends became much less stressful. But other changes to balance requirements did subpostmasters no favours. At the time of our appointment, we were allowed to cancel three post office balances a year - as long as the request was made in writing at least two weeks in advance. This was useful as few substitutes were prepared to tackle the weekly nightmare. The only balances that couldn't be cancelled were those at a period end and as a period at the time was a quarter,, there were only four balances a year that couldn't be cancelled. Now subpostmasters are allowed to cancel only *two* balances a year as long as they don't coincide with a period end. And as a period has now changed from a quarter to a month, there are now *twelve* balances a year that can't be cancelled. Halfway through one holiday, I had to drive back from Pembrokeshire, complete the balance, and then drive back, making us feel we'd had a somewhat fractured break. A few years later we holidayed in Prague, came back at eleven o'clock on the Wednesday night and had the balance to do before we could go to bed. This took some of the gloss off a wonderful break. We vowed never to let this happen again and when two subsequent breaks overlapped a period end, we returned on the Saturday and partially guessed the previous week's balance. Not strictly in accordance with the terms of our contract, I grant you, but a legitimate compromise between the end-of-period accounting regulations and the need for shopkeepers and postmasters to have a break.

When we took over at Poulton, Harold and Jessie volunteered to stand in for us whenever we wanted a break. Harold found it difficult to accept that it was our shop anyway and when he came back he would immediately start fussing around, tidying things that were already (by our standards) tidy, and engaging in a sort of re-colonisation. I was reminded of a variation on the old saying: "You can take a postmaster out of the post office but you can't take the post office out of the postmaster." The postmaster left *us* the day we left the post office - and shows no sign of coming back. But then we were only imposters, playing the role with varying degrees of conviction. Harold was the real thing.

Harold and Jessie took over twice - once after our first Christmas to give us a winter break and the following summer when we spent a week in Cornwall. On each occasion, Harold left a list of "Do's and Don'ts" as long as your arm. And on the second occasion he actually reversed some of our changes - putting the toilet rolls back in the stores - not quite a bus ride away but you get the picture, - and taking down two shelves that I'd had the temerity to put up. He was like one of the Old Colonialists who returned to Africa a few years after Independence and spent their entire visit talking about what the Africans couldn't organise in a brewery and how we should never have handed the country over in the first place. We were grateful for the breaks that Harold and Jessie gave us, but relieved when they said they didn't want the responsibility of doing it any more.

So for more than ten years, whether we had holidays or not depended on Joyce and she never let us down. Mind you, she frequently threatened to. Her reluctance to take responsibility was legendary and whenever we planned a few days off, neither of us was keen to break the news to her. Joyce's typical response - if we hinted that we were planning to go away the following weekend - would be something like: "What a co-incidence. So am I!"

But she always came good in the end and we couldn't have asked for a more reliable stand-in. A previous chapter was called *Minding Your Own Business* but Joyce was extremely good at minding *our* business. Her reluctance was due to her taking the responsibility *too* seriously and putting herself under a great deal of stress while we were away. Other people planning to leave their businesses worry about whether their substitute is honest, competent and reliable. Their worry is how the person will handle the business. Our worry was exactly the opposite; how the business would handle Joyce, and we sold at least one extra bottle of whisky during our absence as she needed a good slug every night to help her sleep. In fairness, we often left her at particularly busy times. The post office frequently experienced queues for motor vehicle licences stretching out into the street and this happened several times when Joyce was in charge. We were left in no doubt how stressful she found it!

Joyce's problem was a lack of faith in her own considerable abilities. She was particularly suspicious of any new transactions and in the later years had sleepless nights over such things as Travel Insurance and Foreign Exchange. Overseas parcels were another of her nightmares. Percy, the ex-postmaster in the nearby town who we asked to "keep an eye on Joyce" while we were away, once teased her at 11.50 on a Saturday by asking if she could cope with six air parcels to Peru.

Because of Joyce we managed one major holiday every year and a few short breaks in between. One of our first holidays was in Skye where we felt thoroughly remote from everything connected with shopkeeping. On the Thursday morning we came across a phone box in a particularly desolate stretch of moorland and for some reason I decided to phone home. I asked Joyce how she was and her reply, "Absolutely knackered", was as predictable as anything in life could be. It put a blight on the rest of the day but what had I expected? Particularly on pensions day.

WHERE ARE MY BLOODY KEYS?!!!

I swore that during our holidays I would never phone home again which makes my decision to do so the following year incomprehensible. Again I dialled the fateful number, again Joyce replied and when she realised who it was barked "Where are my bloody car keys?" Trying to ease her load, I'd put some of the Friday deliveries into her car before we left but had then undone my good work by pocketing her keys. Luckily, she had a spare set at home, although she didn't tell me this immediately.

"Absolutely knackered!" and "Where are my bloody car keys?" At least Joyce could never be accused of hiding her true feelings. I renewed my resolve never to phone home again and this time stuck to it. Just as well as an incident one Saturday morning might have triggered a ripe response. Joyce was running the shop with my son Nick and around mid-morning who should come in but the evil-smelling Miss Cocker.

"I bought some apples here last week," Miss Cocker said. "They were advertised as Cox's but they didn't taste like Cox's to me."

Joyce, overpowered like everyone else by the old woman's aroma, muttered something noncommittal whereupon Miss Cocker delved into her bag and produced a dirty old piece of tissue paper. Wrapped inside was a scrap of yellowy-brown substance, which she identified as a piece of apple.

"Now' she said, all businesslike. "Would you please taste this and tell me whether that apple is a Cox's?"

I'm sure it was only her loyalty to us that prevented Joyce shooting out of the door and never being seen again.

"No I won't," she said. "I don't even eat things after my husband. It's unhygienic."

Undeterred, Miss Cocker swung round and thrust the morsel under Nick's nose. "Then perhaps this young man would like to taste it for me."

Nick paled and managed to shake his head. Child abuse cases have been brought for less. No wonder Joyce was increasingly reluctant for us to go away.

Joyce had a string of assistants none of whom stayed for long. The most resilient was Barbara McIntyre who one afternoon when she was alone in the shop accidentally set off the post office alarm. We had taught Barbara a lot of things about the post office; how to de-activate the alarm wasn't one of them, and she was confronted by a continuous and deafening ringing. She then compounded the problem by locking herself in the post office. All she could think of doing was phoning Joyce who was at home and in the bathroom. Realising she couldn't make herself heard above the noise, Joyce rushed to the shop and, without contravening any post office dress codes (we trust!), rescued Barbara from her predicament.

We never found a truly satisfactory second assistant until Ampney Crucis Post Office closed and we acquired Marlene Broadhurst. Marlene was perfect - cheerful and reliable and providing continuity for those residents of Ampney Crucis who had transferred their business to Poulton. Before Marlene, the closest we came was a woman who lived across the road from the shop, who needed a job, and whose cavalier approach was the perfect foil for Joyce's caution. She was the answer to our prayers but her husband spoiled it all by running off with another woman. A messy divorce followed, the woman left Poulton and we were left to reflect on the utter selfishness of husbands who, by giving in to extramarital temptations, leave their local shopkeepers struggling yet again to arrange their annual break.

PART FOUR

MID-TERM BLUES

CHAPTER ONE.

RUDE AWAKENINGS

Sometimes when I opened the shop in the morning I got a sense of the futility of a shopkeeper's life. As I dealt with what I had come to think of as the "one-item" customers, the words of Prince Hal in Henry IV came to mind:

I know you all and will awhile uphold
The unyoked humour of your idleness.
Therein will I imitate the sun
That doth permit the base, contagious clouds
To smother up his humour from the earth.

While not really seeing myself as a Prince Hal waiting to assume his birthright, there were times, particularly as I dealt with the early morning trade, that I felt I must have been born for something better. I certainly saw the "one-item" brigade as the equivalent of the base contagious clouds.

At 8.40 every morning outside the shop, the same man would be pacing around. At 8.45 I opened, keen to sort out bread orders, vegetable orders, post office problems and sundry telephone calls. I would get the newspaper bags and the milk in and start to organise the post office. This would all be interrupted by the man paying for his *Sun*.

And that was all he ever bought. One 28p newspaper and every morning I interrupted my tasks to take his paltry offering so that he could enjoy the softcore porn and hardcore prejudices of the Murdoch press. Occasionally he would wait, hovering querulously and I'd realise I'd overcharged him. Murdoch, in an attempt to see off his tabloid rivals, sometimes reduced the price of the Sun to 10p and thousands of newsagents had to remember to change their newsbills or face complaints from customers - just another thing to prevent our brains seizing up.

Anyway off he would go with his *Sun* and I would ask myself how he imagined we survived on his daily 28p. Well he obviously didn't imagine. Like so many other villagers, he saw the survival of the shop as nothing he could begin to influence, or even *want* to influence.

But he wasn't alone and a few minutes later another member of the Murdoch Supporters' Club would come along. He was more upmarket, at least in his reading. He took *The Times*.. No Page 3 girls for him but then his wife - a staunch pillar of the church - wouldn't have allowed it. His usual topic of conversation, apart from some soundbite like "Bring back the birch" or "All Arabs are the same", was the weather. Occasionally he would lament the way our politicians were surrendering power to Brussels oblivious to the irony of his support for an Australian-born American doing all he could to corner the British communications market, one of whose publications claimed to have been a decisive factor in the last two general elections. On Mondays he also paid 10p - the price of the *Times* was reduced to undercut the other broadsheets. And *he* never bought anything else either.

Reading through this, it sounds as if on these mornings I was consumed by bitterness. I wasn't - at least not *consumed* by it. There was enough humour, enough genuine customers, enough enchantment to most days to preclude bitterness. And anyway, some bitterness comes with the territory, is part of a shopkeeper's life.

But I did occasionally muse over the future of the shop and wondered how long it could survive to provide newspaper and post office services for people who never used it for anything else. I wondered why so many people in the village seemed obsessed by the idea of *not* using us for anything else. We weren't pariahs (were we?); our shop wasn't *so* bad (was it?). It couldn't have been; it won the Gloucestershire Village Shop of the Year award in 1996. And even after that, the same people *still* didn't use us.

Why not? They needed teabags, bread, sugar, milk, toilet paper. Why was it that a complete cross section of the local community, from landed gentry to farm labourers, used us and a far bigger cross-section of the same local community didn't use us at all. Yet when we saw them it was always "Stuart and Liz" as though we were all bosom pals. It was a puzzle to which we never found a satisfactory answer other than the glib "Village shops are too expensive." Perhaps after all it *was* only a matter of economics. Perhaps it really *was* that simple.

Lunchtime was our watershed, when I came down from my study, put the kettle on and informed Lizzie that it was time to close the shop. The hour from one to two was the most precious of the day. Customers who came in at 12.58 with three motor vehicle licences didn't appreciate the value of the time they were using up. At five thirty it was no problem. Then we closed for the night - what did a few extra minutes matter? But those few minutes at one o'clock were gold dust.

After I started getting up at what I always insisted was an ungodly hour to do the papers, I compensated by having a lunchtime sleep and Lizzie, never one to miss the chance of a nap, decided to join me. She once sent me a Valentine card saying "I would lie in bed all day if I could *dream of you*," with the last three words crossed out. So after a quick lunch, we would retire. Sometimes the time in bed was as little as ten minutes. Usually it was nearer forty but, ten or forty, it didn't matter. The nap was the great divide, the great reviver. We would sleep through the *World at One* and *The Archers* and finally emerge from the Land of Nod during the Shipping Forecast, gradually surfacing as the announcer reeled off those strange place names. To us, the Shipping Forecast wasn't information for all those souls drifting around on the high seas but a litany of names during which we mentally prepared ourselves to face the afternoon. Just past the halfway point, the broadcaster changed to "Weather reports from Coastal Stations" and I knew I should be getting up. "Rising slowly" was often appended to the reports and sometimes I wasn't rising at all. Occasionally I dozed off again and heard the voice say "Channel Light Vessel Automatic". Now I had to rise very rapidly indeed. I would shoot out of bed and peek through the curtains as I pulled on my trousers. Sometimes a car had drawn up and a couple of people would be waiting outside. One customer who was always there on a certain day we unaccountably called 'bollock breeches.' "And finally Jersey" the voice would say as I pulled on my sweater realising that I still had nothing on my feet. "It should be finally shoes," I thought as I did up the laces.

"And finally Jersey."

I heard the dreaded phrase a split second before Lizzie dug me in the ribs. The shipping forecaster had got round to the Channel Isles and I was still in bed.

"It's two o'clock. We've overslept."

I shot out of bed like a scalded cat and in a blur of limbs, trousers, shirt and shoes broke the world getting dressed record. Taking the stairs four at a time, I rushed to the shop just as the first impatient rattlings were starting on the door. I fumbled in my pocket for the keys only to find I'd left them in the bedroom. Not the ideal end to our lunchtime period of tranquillity.

After the two o'clock rush, on some bleak days in January and February, we'd have hardly any customers until maybe half past three. Sometimes I'd retire to the lounge and sit near the fire, leaving the adjoining door open. It was never relaxing. After a long bleak period, the shop door would suddenly open, a stranger would come in, proffer a twenty-pound note and ask for a box of matches. At various times in my life, I've wondered which of the ten commandments was the most difficult to keep but as I went through the ritual of unlocking the post office door, producing the box of matches and giving him his £19.90 change, I had little doubt. "Thou shalt not kill" - the most difficult by a mile.

Some of you - the older ones - might remember the song "Tuesday Afternoon" on the first Moody Blues Album, Justin Hayward et al presenting it as a time of glorious release. He'd obviously never been in charge of a village post office. Tuesday afternoons - particularly those dismal Tuesdays in the middle of winter - were less a time of release than a time of captivity when for a couple of hours the shop fulfilled neither its social nor its commercial function - no customers to talk to, no money in the till. If we'd ever decided to walk out of the shop and never come back, it would surely have happened on one of those wintry Tuesday afternoons.

Tuesday afternoons in summer were never as bad except during Wimbledon when the whole of Poulton came to a standstill. I'd stand poised neurotically between the shop and the TV room, watching a critical match between two tennis aces. (Never a British player of course, in those days. Jeremy Bates - our one hope for the second round - had already gone - a brave rearguard action against the Namibian No.5 ending in four sets). I would watch an enthralling five setter build to its climax, and at match point the shop door would open and a delivery man would enter wanting to know the way to Priory court, Poulton Grange, the Owl House or any of the myriad places which saw us as their personal locational aids. Reluctantly I would give him directions - and some of those guys are so thick you wonder if they're safe to be on the road in the first place (So, second on the left was it? No, first on the right. Left at the pub? No, right at the pub. What was all that about Down something or other? Down Ampney and I said straight through. Straight through what?) I'd usher him out of the shop - still doing some calculation on his fingers and looking thoroughly disorientated - and rush back to the telly, to find as likely as not that the match had ended. (I suddenly realise as I write this that for all future summers I can watch the whole of Wimbledon, the open golf, and the test matches, to my heart's content. In future, Tuesday afternoons will mean to me what they meant to the Moody Blues all those years ago!)

Lizzie meanwhile was often watching Wimbledon untroubled by anything except her conscience. Our arrangement was that I opened the shop in the mornings, she took over around ten, and I did most of the afternoons. To compensate for my early mornings (even in times of dire illness, I would struggle downstairs and get the papers sorted reflecting that it took more than a killer virus to disturb our newspaper delivery service) she decided to take over the management of the post office - doing the balance, ordering the stock and mugging up on new transaction types. In addition she did almost all the shop ordering, (I dealt with the cash and carry in our final years) the ironing, the cleaning, the parenting, the gardening, and most of the cooking. I reckon I got a good deal by doing the newspapers - even when I had to do a round in winter - but she still considered it a fair swop. You can see how much she likes her bed in the morning. I should add that I did almost all the writing and played most of the golf just in case anybody thinks I got *too* good a deal.

Joking apart, it was a good partnership. I controlled the cash flow and the banking, paid the bills, and did quite a lot of teaching. We each had a full life, contributing more or less equally to the partnership.

How Rob managed when the Post Office deprived him of his lunchtime break, I don't know. Without the one o'clock watershed, he had to play the full ninety minutes, as it were, straight off. Customers sometimes asked why *we* didn't open lunchtimes. "It'd be much more convenient," they'd say. "We'd use you a lot more. By the time we get here, it's after one and you're closed." Well for a time Rob did open lunchtimes and I asked him how often Mrs A, Miss B, and Mr C had taken advantage of the new opening times. "Not once," was his unsurprising reply. The amount of extra business he attracted by staying open between one and two was negligible and the Post Office, astonishingly accepting his case, allowed him to revert to the previous opening hours.

I had a reputation for being somewhat stressed towards the end of the day. A sort of five o'clock shadow passed over me and I changed from the good-humoured Stuart Jekyl and grew tufts of hair and elongated canines. Well, what did people expect? Having drifted aimlessly through most of the afternoon, serving the odd customer, filling a few shelves, generally doing my best to stave off boredom, I would be totally unprepared when, at five, the shop suddenly resembled a Californian town in the gold rush. And as we never believed in using two people even if the shop needed two, I tried to cope on my own. And cope I did - usually - sticking on stamps, selling cigarettes, slicing ham, weighing potatoes while all the time trying to fulfil the terms of my subpostmaster's contract by completing the "end of day" documentation so that the official envelopes could all go off with the postman. I coped by giving an impression of a bluebottle and as long as nobody expected me to exude happiness while I was coping. And if during those frantic half-hours, I occasionally resembled John Cleese playing Mr. Hide, all I can say is I never actually bit anyone.

So what if I became a little stressed after five o'clock? Serving customers, dealing with post *and* doing the post office accounts in the full glare of the public eye is not a situation designed to lower the blood pressure. How many other professionals do their accounts to comments like "Bit slow today, isn't he? Only been waiting ten minutes. Never mind he'll serve us sooner or later." etc. etc. etc.? Most accounts are done behind closed doors with a minimum of distraction. Ours were done between issuing a motor vehicle licence, selling a bottle of wine and giving somebody directions - almost certainly to Priory Court.

"Why do you leave everything till the last minute?" a woman asked me icily one afternoon when she had been waiting perhaps two minutes for a first class stamp. I glared at her and bit my lip, waiting for the inspired put down that never came. If it had, I might have said, "Madam, if it wasn't for the last minute nothing would ever get done."

But after half past five, our time was our own, as well as all the food in the shop and the wine on the shelves. One aspect of Harold's stewardship that we totally approved of was his belief in minimal opening hours. Extending the time the business was open to the public was one aspect of its potential that we had no desire whatsoever to exploit.

And Rob surely reflects as he sits down around six with a glass of his Wine of the Month, how much better it all is than being stuck in a traffic jam on the M4 or waiting on a cold wet station for a train that is forty minutes late. He must think as we did that running a village shop has more than its share of compensations.

Even though, for a time, the Post Office made him give up his lunchtimes.

CHAPTER TWO

BITTER SHOPKEEPERS.

Make no mistake about it, shopkeepers do become bitter. Lizzie and I avoided it on the whole - a dry cynicism was as far as we went - but for many, bitterness comes with the territory. We would see them at the cash and carry, grey and humourless, eyes never raised from the treadmill of their existence. I used to encourage customers from neighbouring villages to support their local shop - if they still had one. One claimed she tried but explained that "when I leave *your* shop, I feel happy, when I leave the shop in *my* village, I feel depressed." So bitterness becomes a way of life and a downward spiral. Shopkeepers become bitter through lack of trade. Their bitterness affects the customers they *do* have and they go elsewhere. Trade then drops further and the bitterness increases.

One regularly displayed signs in the village saying, "The village shop will close next month if things don't improve." He gave more ultimatums than the boy who cried wolf and after a time nobody believed them. Another would suddenly decide to close the shop mid-morning putting up a sign saying "Closed through lack of customers." The only people to suffer were the people who actually *wanted* to use the shop and found it closed. He became so embittered that he wouldn't let people post letters in his post-box unless they'd bought the stamps at his post office. You see what dark, vindictive waters shopkeepers' minds drift around in.

As I said, we avoided sliding into bitterness although the attitude of a few "customers" sometimes drove us to the edge. There was a woman who always greeted us as if we were among her most intimate acquaintances, claimed to value the shop, came in regularly to use the post office, spent time looking round, and then asked us for something we hadn't got. And this happened too often for it to be anything but a planned strategy. On one occasion she looked at our booze shelves and, seeing the empty space where cider should have been, asked for some cider.

But this time I was ready for her. I dashed round the back and emerged in my Basil Fawlty pose with two bottles. Her face fell.

"I wanted Bulmer's."

"This is Bulmer's."

"I wanted dry."

"This is dry."

She thought for a moment, then, quick as a flash, asked "Do you have it in cans?" And when I shook my head, she shook hers and put on her "What a shame" expression. "I don't know what it is but cider never tastes quite the same in bottles."

I quit, acknowledging defeat at the hands of a master. The woman had elevated not using the shop into an art form.

But at least she realised that she *should* be using the shop even though in reality she had no intention of ever doing so. Several other people used the shop for emergency purchases perhaps once a month and showed no conscience whatsoever about giving it so little support. A case in point was a man who never bought anything except a paper on Saturday. He was always a few pence short and after helping himself to the paper would yell out to whoever happened to be serving "I'll owe you the rest." One Saturday morning, this got too much for Lizzie who refused to let him have the paper. There was protracted correspondence during which both he and his wife completely failed to understand that the money (I think it was 4p) wasn't the issue. The issue was taking for granted a privilege, which we readily gave to people who asked and who generally gave us support. Needless to say we never saw the couple again and I can only say it was their loss. They joined Mr. Minnow and the woman who thought we were meddling in her finances among the very few villagers who refused to use the shop due to a basic disagreement or misunderstanding.

Then there was the woman who only ever bought the *Wilts and Glos. Standard*. It was always delivered on a Thursday evening and although I billed her every month, she would call in the shop to pay perhaps once a year. (We should really have stopped deliveries but we were always loath to take such a measure). When she made her annual visit, she would invariably dispute the bill saying she owed for thirty eight papers not thirty nine and the bill should therefore be £12.20, not £12.60. What could I do, except admire the arithmetical certainty in a woman of such advanced years?

One customer even objected to licking her own stamps. She suspected the glue was toxic and wanted me to lick them for her - it was apparently all right for the subpostmaster to be poisoned. The Post Office has been accused of many things but being a sort of bureaucratic Dr. Crippen isn't one of them – yet.

There was another man who had made a career out of prudence. He spent a large part of the year overseas and always knew where the currency had collapsed and where the best deals were to be had. We were regaled with stories of apartments in Bucharest where £5 would get you seats at the opera plus a candlelit dinner for two with a girl thrown in. He never bought anything apart from the *Times* - when it was reduced in price - and an occasional punnet of strawberries in summer. Mind you, a man who reputedly rocked his first marriage by complaining about the amount of toothpaste his bride was using on her honeymoon night was hardly likely to pay the slightly higher prices charged in his local shop.

A few customers objected to what we came to think of as "the Sunday charge". We started selling Sunday papers when the man who had sold them in the nearby bus shelter for several years decided he'd had enough. Against some of our most deeply held principles (i.e. shopkeepers, like God, deserve one day a week to themselves) and to keep the facility in the village, we started opening for two hours on Sunday mornings. To cover our costs - employing Marlene and paying W.H.Smith's delivery charge - we continued the previous practice of adding 5p to the cost of each newspaper. Most customers accepted this without question. A few complained. After a few months, one woman - who I now think of as Mrs Fivepence - asked us to justify the 5p. I explained that it was to cover our extra expenses on Sunday but she wasn't convinced. I pointed out that there was no compulsion to pay it as no one was forcing her to buy her paper from the shop. However, a trip to the nearest alternative newsagent's would take about half an hour and £1's worth of petrol. She was of course perfectly free to take up this option.

I mention this not because of the sum involved but because it shows how irrational people can be in their dealings with the shop. Mrs Fivepence never used the shop for anything other than her newspapers. She seemed to view the shop the way people view the war memorial - wonderful that the village had one as long as she didn't have to do anything about its upkeep. What, pay 5p willingly and uncomplainingly for the excellent service the shop provides in bringing Sunday papers to the village? Not if I can help it.

As I said only a few people complained about the Sunday charge. One man, on hearing of the charge, fixed Marlene with a suspicious glare and immediately cancelled his paper. Forever.

I can do no better than quote Bill Bryson's *Notes from a Small Island.* "I may not agree with what you're doing but I will defend to the death your right to behave like a complete asshole." It is after all a free country. If you wish to forego the dubious pleasure of reading the *Mail on Sunday* because you object to your shopkeepers covering their costs with a surcharge that is a quarter of the price of one cigarette, that is your democratic right. We are committed to defending the rights of all minorities even when, as in this case, the minority is very small indeed.

As I've indicated elsewhere some customers did treat us a bit like a public convenience. If only we had ten pounds for every person who entered the shop with the words "Sorry to trouble you but..." We live in an age when no professional person gives anything for nothing. I mentioned earlier the accountant who charged us for a meeting and for advice given at the meeting. I once had several telephone conversations with the bank manager about my overdraft - conversations with the bank manager were always about my overdraft – and was horrified when the quarterly statement of bank charges came through to see that, in addition to interest, business charges and a charge for setting up the overdraft, I'd also been charged £41 for management time. Does he have any idea how long it took us to earn that amount of money? It seems that none of the large banks has any real concept of putting the customer first. Excluding the privatised utilities, they are perhaps the only enterprises that continue making huge profits irrespective of the economic climate and when I hear descriptions of banks as "listening" and "caring" I can only smile at the unintentional irony.

But the village shopkeeper *is* listening and caring. He usually likes being these things; whether he does or not he frequently has to be. And much of what he spends his day doing is in fact unpaid and perhaps in some cases unappreciated. We knew virtually every house and every occupant in the village so naturally the post office was the place to come when strangers (usually delivery men) needed directions. On average, we responded a dozen times a day to such requests. Sometimes it happened even when the shop was closed and the inquiries came to the house. Villagers on the whole respected our privacy and our need for time off (some might say too much time off) but even during off-duty hours we were still fair game for strangers seeking directions.

The village shopkeeper has to accept that he is there to be made use of; to receive parcels for villagers who may be out when the postman calls; to have bundles of mail deposited on him by local businesses; to give directions ad nauseam to visitors of all descriptions who are strangers to the area. He is there to do all these things, not only because it is expected of him but also because he is concerned with building up goodwill. The public doesn't distinguish between the shop and the proprietors and if the proprietors are seen as unco-operative, the shop will lose custom. Therefore it's important both for the village and his own financial well-being that the shopkeeper gets a reputation for being amenable even though he may occasionally have to bite his tongue. It certainly ill behoves him to create ill-will as, in the words of the old saying, "bad news has breasted the tape before good news has its running shoes on" and the ripple effect of one dissatisfied customer will probably mean that more than that one customer is lost. The cynical view - and one that we could never subscribe to! - is that before you treat anyone badly ensure that they are neither too popular nor too influential.

On the whole, customers are pretty sensitive - with some notable exceptions. These are the one-item customers, the "sorry to trouble you" customers, the "we wouldn't be here if we could get to the supermarket " customers, the "have you got change for the phone, the car park or the cigarette machine?" customers.

Our worst example of insensitivity - worse even than the woman who wanted to leave her supermarket shopping in our freezer - was a chap who asked us to distribute some leaflets. We agreed - assuming he wouldn't be advertising sex, drugs, or pornographic literature. We were right. He was advertising something much worse - the free bus to the new Tesco superstore. We told him politely what he could do with his leaflets and he had the nerve to storm off, quite aggrieved that a couple of turkeys had refused to help him plan the Christmas menu.

CHAPTER THREE

PREJUDICE.

There are many statues of men slaying lions but if the lions had been the sculptors, we might have a different set of statues. (Aesop)

The papers were full of the massacre of the Egyptian tourists near the temple of Hatchipsut in the Valley of the Kings. Innocent seekers after culture and beauty mowed down by terrorists with an utterly misguided sense of what constitutes justice, or how they might gain the attention - and the sympathy - of the world.

As I opened the shop and started my chores, one of the early morning customers came in, a woman who embodied a particular strain of bleak sourness. On Tuesdays she bought the *Radio Times* but always tore off the cover (a blanket prejudice against anyone who appeared on the cover of the Radio Times was one of her less disagreeable features).

"Dreadful about those people in Egypt," I ventured as Noel Edmonds or some such buffoon disappeared into the waste bin.

"Serves them right for going to a place like that."

I wondered if my ears were playing tricks. Serves them right? For going to a place like that? Even by the standards of justice espoused by the extreme right, this was breaking new ground. Egypt was obviously high on her list of places not to visit. For going to such a place, a reasonable punishment was to be massacred.

I tried again. "I went to Egypt. I thought it was wonderful."

"I've never been and I wouldn't want to go." And that seemed to be the end of that. Egypt was one of those places peopled by lesser forms of humanity and anybody who went there deserved all they got.

It shouldn't have surprised me. Pockets of racism are alive and well in the Cotswolds. I had one customer say, when discussing

Saddam Hussein, "All Arabs are the same." Another explained how he got round the equal opportunity laws. "If I advertise a job and a black comes to inquire about it, I tell him it's gone. It hasn't; I just tell him it has."

After the 1998 World Cup and the shame of David Beckham, a woman brought up the subject of the wages of Premiership footballers. I said I thought it was ridiculous that Beckham, exceptional player though he was, should be paid £12,000 a week or whatever the figure was at the time. Her response was, "Well that Paul Ince gets £10,000 a week - and he's black!"

What can you say to such people? What can you say to someone who has lived in a multi-racial democracy for perhaps forty years and still can't accept black people being treated as equals? I too think it's a scandal that Paul Ince is paid £10,000 a week. My impression is that he's not a particularly nice man who has a chip on his shoulder. But this has nothing to do with his being black. I should add that we didn't encounter prejudice like this very often and I'm sure the number of bigots in Poulton is very small. Most residents are urbane people of a liberal persuasion who would be appalled to know that such outmoded attitudes persisted in our village.

But we live in an age of prejudices - racism, sexism, ageism, and countless others. Lizzie and I are untainted by such irrationality and don't actually have prejudices – well perhaps Lizzie has the odd one. All our attitudes are based on careful reasoning and logic. We served anyone in our shop - black or white, male or female, old or young, upper, middle or lower class, straight or gay, right-handed or left-handed. Our only point of discrimination was between people who spent money with us and those who didn't, between customers and non-customers. So I suppose in modern jargon we were "customerists", judging people not by the colour of their skin, but by the colour of their money, by their retail rather than their sexual orientation. Compulsive and exclusive supermarket users were the retail equivalent of sexual deviants.

Running a village shop causes a suspension of usual moral values. I'd be the last person to say that people who live in a village and don't use their shop should be shot (actually I'd be the first but for the sake of argument we'll pretend I'd be the last) but it was certainly hard not to let it colour our judgement of them. I used to joke that if Hitler had lived in the village, we'd have judged him solely on whether he used the shop. At least people thought it was a joke – I'm not entirely sure. (We'd probably have drawn the line at Michael Howard).

It was only after we left the shop that we could develop normal relationships. One evening at a concert, we were in the company of an institutionalised non-shop user and, to our surprise, found that she was really quite a nice person.

But to prove how strong our retail orientation became, consider the following episode. Our time in the shop brought us into contact with a lot of people, many of them members of the Conservative Party. As with Milo Minderbinder in *Catch 22*, we didn't mind who we did deals with as long as they paid. "Are you selling things to the enemy again?" I could imagine K.M., that well-known Poulton Socialist saying as he saw me delivering an order to the house of Mrs Round. "And why not?" I would have retorted. "At least they support us which is more than can be said for some of our so-called allies."

Mrs Round was a big noise in the local Tory party and one of our village shop loyalists. In the eighties, the local MP was Nicholas Ridley, Old Nick himself, and Mrs Round introduced him to us just before the 1987 General Election. The most memorable part of his visit was his total disregard of the no smoking notices as he puffed away all the time he was in the shop. Perhaps he didn't know he was breaking the rules or, more likely, he didn't care. Is it any wonder that the public opinion of politicians is so low when the Minister of State for the Environment shows such disregard for the accepted standards of behaviour?

But we did have one reason to be grateful to Nicholas Ridley. As Minister of Transport, and because he was a friend of Harold, he arranged for Poulton Post Office to sell motor vehicle licences which by the time we took over formed a substantial part of our post office trade. It is unusual for a small office to have this facility and completely unfair on all the other small offices in the area. But we weren't complaining.

Mrs Round brought Old Nick into the shop to ask for our support not knowing that he was unlikely to get it. We said we were Liberals - well, we were in the eighties, that heady time of mould-breaking and the two Davids. Admitting to voting Liberal was sort of *half* a confession, the last outpost on the road towards political unacceptability. We dared not admit to being Labour voters - Ridley might have closed us down. It was a bit like the situation I faced at university when I confessed to my tutor how little work I'd done and asked him whether I should make the same confession to the Professor. "NOOOO!" he yelled in panic. "Just confess a bit of it!" Admitting to voting Liberal was confessing a bit of it.

From then on Mrs Round treated us with a smiling paternalism. We may not have been "one of us" but we certainly weren't one of them. Unlike Harold, who *was* "one of us" but who she obviously found irritating. One day, her phone had been cut off. She hadn't paid the first bill, but had paid when BT sent their usual reminder. However, something had gone wrong and she came to the post office to ask Harold what had happened. "If you'd paid the first bill you wouldn't have been cut off," Harold told her, whereupon Mrs

Round hit the roof. "Don't you dare pass judgement on my bill-paying," she informed him. "It's none of your business whether I pay my first bill, my second bill or whether I pay at all!" And quite right too. We are administrators of the system, not its custodians. People used to apologise for being late with all kinds of bills as though they expected us to pass moral judgement or even inform the authorities.

The Chairman of the local branch of the Tory party was a certain Mr Cheese, a quietly-spoken defender of the faith, always charming, always polite and with a steely determination never to use the village shop.

Except for one thing. When the Tories were organising a function, he always bought his wine from us. This ritual stemmed from a day at the beginning of our tenure when we had Liebfraumilch on special offer. Those of you who know your German will translate Liebfraumilch as something like "Dear Lady's Milk" or perhaps "the drink for your sweetheart." Those who know your wine will realise it's not really the drink for your worst enemy, let alone your sweetheart. (Christ's miracle might have earned substantially fewer kudos if he'd turned water into Liebfraumilch). But Mr Cheese bought a bottle and fastened on to it as one of the wines of the century. "Are you going to have any more of that very good wine?" he'd say on his rare visits to the shop. On being reassured that we were, he would go away, a look of beatific contentment on his face.

So for Conservative party functions he always bought the wine from us - twelve bottles of the "very good wine" and twelve bottles of an Italian red called Valpolicella, another "very good wine". When he first started serving these at Tory get-togethers, we thought he'd be out on his ear. Surely the local Tories would be able to tell the quality of a wine when it hit their palettes and on tasting the wine served by Mr Cheese, might think it was a left-wing plot to poison them. Not a bit of it. Liebfraumilch and Valpolicella went down extremely well and lubricated every subsequent Tory gathering.

But we were always grateful for Mr Cheese's patronage and hope that our surprise at his choice of wine will be seen as a back-handed compliment. We expected him and his fellow Tories to have more sophisticated palates. But at least he bought the wine from the village shop. Which again was more than could be said for some of our allies.

CHAPTER FOUR

IN SHEEP'S CLOTHING

Most of our suppliers were first class. They gave excellent service and had a good sense of humour. These were generally the smaller suppliers. The larger ones had sacs of neat venom in their filofaxes - used sparingly but with devastating effect.

All right, let's name names. I'm talking in particular about Londis and the Danish Bacon Company though the drivers, with one or two exceptions, couldn't have been friendlier or more co-operative. One exception was a driver who showed little under-standing of the concepts of gravity, compression or thoroughfare and when unloading our deliveries blocked all routes through the shop with precarious piles of obstructions built with the smallest or the least resistant package at the bottom. Another was the newspaper delivery driver who screeched to a halt around five o'clock every morning with pop music blaring at a thousand deci-bels. He hurled the packages against the shop door and screeched off like a Formula One driver as a few villagers stirred uneasily in their beds and wondered why the Martians should have chosen Poulton for their invasion point. But these drivers were just irri-tants, standing out because of the contrast with their fellow drivers who were generally beyond reproach. We can't say the same for the companies they worked for.

Londis was our first disappointment. And the disappointment was greater because they'd given such reassurance when we took over. Harold arranged for us to meet the rep during our first week when we bought our two mandatory £50 shares. We listened to him describe the company's commitment to "the little men" in such emotional terms that a tear rolled down my cheek and Jessie played an imaginary violin behind his back. But at least we were under the wing of a company who would deliver the goods (in every way) and the scenario of twice weekly trips to the cash and carry wouldn't materialise, at least not for a few years. By the time it did, we were prepared for them and they were nowhere near as traumatic as we had feared.

But Londis were perfect - or so we thought. And we continued to think them perfect for several years until one day we had another visit from our guardian angel. Only this time he seemed more like a debt collector as he explained that our business was too small for Londis to continue deliveries. He gave us three months to double our orders or unfortunately....

He didn't finish the sentence. He didn't need to. We were being jettisoned. The fairy godmother had become a whore, selling herself to the highest bidder. The guardian angel had exchanged her wings for a snakeskin.   Three months to double our trade! If we'd been capable of that, we'd have been *running* Londis and headhunted by every retailer in the land. So three months later Londis abandoned us along with other similar businesses and the Danish Bacon Company, following in their wake, found the Humpty Dumpties lying on the ground and helped their owners put them together again.

DBC really *were* our guardian angels. Like a jilted lover, we were over the moon to start another relationship so quickly and had little doubt that this was finally what we had been looking for. No minimum orders, deliveries when we wanted them, reasonable profit margins, no delivery charge (unlike Londis) and around four weeks credit - give or take a few days. We'd found a supplier that suited us down to the ground. And we carried on thinking so for about six years.

Then one day we received a letter from Head Office informing us that our period of credit was being reduced from four weeks to ten days. And this was to come into effect not at some point in the future but from our next order. They were depriving us of three weeks' credit at a stroke which meant we had to find a thousand pounds almost immediately. Even Londis had given us three months. Was this another innocent being seduced by the wicked ways of the world of commerce and finding village shops too homely for her newly-acquired sophistication?

We hoped not and felt that our standing with DBC was sufficient not to require immediate compliance. We had traded with them for a long time, our orders (according to the driver) were the largest he delivered, we had never had cheques returned or credit outstanding beyond the agreed period. DBC had always been sympathetic to our cash-flow problems and even took post-dated cheques in payment.

Not any more.

This was brought home to us the following Wednesday when we phoned in our order. DBC phoned back refusing to accept it until payment for the previous order had been received. I offered to give the driver a post-dated cheque when he delivered on the Friday but was told this was unacceptable. We had two days to find £800 or the order wouldn't be delivered. After a bit of scraping around, it was agreed that I would give the driver £500 in cash and a cheque for the remainder.

The order was delivered on Friday afternoon and when I went to pay, I discovered that Lizzie had gone to town with our only chequebook. I didn't know when she'd be back and told the driver I'd put a cheque in the post that evening. Looking very unhappy, he phoned the company and was told that either I gave him the cheque or the order had to be returned.

Thoroughly bewildered I phoned the company myself. I explained the situation again and said I would put a cheque in the post. I literally couldn't believe it when, after consulting the manager, the girl repeated that a cheque had to be given to the driver. She then had another word with the driver who told me he was under instructions to reload the order.

By now I was jumping up and down with indignation and said that the order would be reloaded over my dead body and the driver had no option but to wait until Lizzie returned. He had no quarrel with me and could see how irrationally the company was behaving. I gave him a cup of tea and a bottle of wine for his trouble.

Naturally, this marked the final chapter - a completely unexpected final chapter - in our relationship with another of the small shops' "guardian angels." Even now I find it incredible that long-standing customers whose dealings with the company had always been beyond reproach should have been treated as serial debtors and denied the right to put a cheque in the post - particularly as we ran a post office. The cheque would have arrived by the following Monday at the latest and couldn't have been banked before then even if the driver had delivered it. The company obviously didn't trust me to keep my word.

I wrote to them hoping for an apology. It was a vain hope and we stopped dealing with them. We forfeited deliveries and they lost a reliable customer but they didn't seem particularly concerned and made no effort to change our minds. We were after all just another small shop, not too difficult to jettison as the blood flowed faster and richer through the veins of these large wholesalers. They may have been slow starters, but like all cold-blooded carnivores, when they feel the sun of increased profits on their backs, watch out! The story of small shops and their battles with larger competitors and suppliers is a parable of our times. Of course the larger organisations have the power to do what they want. It's just that much of what they do, while perfectly legal, comes very close to the border of what is ethical. A system where the weakest go to the wall is not the true hallmark of a civilised society, whether it's achieved by force or finance. Society and business arrangements should be founded on deeper principles than legal requirements.

We'll continue on a happier note. Large suppliers were in fact a rarity during our time in the shop and we used as many small local suppliers as we could. Our original greengrocer was from the nearby town of Fairford - until he became besotted with network marketing, closed his shop and sold his soul to Amway. We found a replacement in Cirencester. Our bread also came from Cirencester, our sausages, bacon and ham from an award-winning butcher in Fairford, our better quality biscuits and up-market jams and pickles from Bristol, our cheese from Ashton Keynes. All these suppliers had three things in common; they were small, they were comparatively local, and they were absolutely accommodating. We miss them as much as we miss our customers and they were one of the reasons for our period in the shop being such a happy one. There *are* business people with both a sense of humour and a soul, two characteristics that our larger suppliers often claimed but seldom displayed when the chips were down.

The driver we had most contact with was a huge man called Pedro, (the one who offered to help during my spat with Mr Minnow). Pedro originally drove for Hilliers, the cold meats and pies company, but he was recycled several times, turning up first with frozen foods, and then ice cream. Hilliers, in fact, had a regular turnover of drivers, the most amusing being George, a Goan chap with a delightful sense of humour. Pedro had recently married a rather large girl called Maria. One day George noticed Pedro give Maria's backside a squeeze and couldn't resist saying: "Cor, Pedro, it's a good job you've got big 'ands." One day George had his van stolen and the police traced it by following a trail of half-eaten pasties and pork pies to a clearing in a forest where the thieves having gorged themselves all night were being violently sick. On another occasion, George left our delivery in a box outside the back door, out of sight of the public but very much in sight of our dog who must have thought all his birthdays had arrived together. But the Hillier's order proved too much even for *his* gargantuan appetite and for weeks we came across packs of half-eaten sausages and mouldy old pies that he'd scattered to all corners of the garden.

We even miss our bread deliverymen even though they arrived before eight thirty and disturbed our breakfast. One of them never worked out how to get the bread trays through the door. He'd start at the midway point, lower the tray to the floor, then raise it to head height oblivious to the fact that the opening was the same width all the way up. He reminded me of our dog trying to work out how to climb the garden steps. Every morning I told him to tilt the tray diagonally but he never got it right. Neither did he last long in the job.

During our final years, our main supplier was Nurdin and Peacock, the cash and carry wholesalers. Nurdin and Peacock (later taken over by Booker) is one of those prefabricated structures that must have been the result of a design-an-appalling-building competition and situated in just about the least attractive area of Gloucester. Off the by-pass, left at the Cheltenham and Gloucester Building Society, through two sets of traffic lights, and suddenly there you were in the industrial sector of East Berlin. To start with we objected to paying on the nail and having to load and transport the goods ourselves until somebody pointed out that this was precisely what cash and carry meant. The staff were efficient and polite and always ready for a laugh. Once when a palette of beer had fallen from a great height on to the driver of a forklift truck and only the protective covering had saved him from serious injury, one of his colleagues remarked "He'll do anything for a drink, that bloke." And they always accepted unquestioningly the return of any stock we'd bought in error. Lizzie used to have nightmares about being locked in - one of those horror film experiences when the heroine suddenly realises she's trapped for the night in a labyrinthine structure with a serial killer stalking the aisles.

I never saw it quite like that. To me it was a treasure trove, a retailer's Aladdin's Cave where all sorts of goodies were available *and could go through the books.* VAT free and set against income tax! I picked up tapes, CDs and clothes in addition to the occasional 'Crazy Clearance' line, once buying a pair of jeans for £2.99. When we went to Prague I disported myself in my new £200 overcoat wearing gloves and a scarf that had cost 49p and 79p respectively. The cafe was a haven of unhealthy options - and I always felt I'd earned an unhealthy option or two after a trip to the cash and carry. Bacon butties, eggs, chips and beans, and at Christmas a greasy turkey dinner. These were my business lunches, my perks, one of the things that made my heart leap just a little at the thought of a cash and carry trip. I say *my* heart as even when she'd got over her initial trepidation, Lizzie never took quite such a rosy view of it. I think she saw it as a slightly up market charity shop. I offered to take her to the cafe for her fiftieth birthday treat but she wasn't keen.

But she enjoyed buying olive oil in bulk, and having a selection of wines and cheeses different from those we sold in the shop. It was just a little depressing to see some of the other worn-down shopkeepers with trolleys loaded with cigarettes, fizzy drinks, crisps and confectionery, evidence of the average Briton's appetite for the unhealthy options and the propensity of small grocers to supply them.

CHAPTER SEVEN

RED TAPE

"Hell hath no fury like a bureaucrat scorned." *(Milton Friedman)*

"Work expands so as to fill the time available for its completion." *(C.Northcote Parkinson).*

A few months ago, there was a worrying report on the *Today* programme about an insidious plant called Japanese Knotweed which grows under houses forcing its way through walls and undermining foundations. (It was particularly worrying for us as the place of the latest attack was Swansea where we own two houses. The problem is so serious that Swansea City Council has appointed a Japanese Knotweed Officer - I'm not joking). It causes evacuations, reduces decent dwellings to the level of wrecks, and is virtually unstoppable. I leave you to deduce why this apparently irrelevant snippet is placed at the beginning of this chapter.

As the extension to our retirement cottage was being built, we found whole swathes of new building and safety regulations that had been introduced during the previous three years. "All related to the comfort and safety of the residents," I was told by a benign building inspector.

Later I considered what he'd said. As the new regulations were mandatory, the logical implication of his remarks was that all buildings erected before the last three years were uncomfortable and unsafe. And, given that such regulations are a never-ending continuum, these current paradigms of comfort and safety would themselves soon be uncomfortable and unsafe. Even as it stood, some parts of our cottage were safe and other parts unsafe. And in a reckless disregard for self-preservation, I am writing this in a part built before 1998.

"We don't want to sanction buildings that are unsafe," the inspector said when I raised the point.

"You mean I'm not safe in the main part of the house."

"Of course you are."

"But that part was built before these new regulations were in place and therefore, according to your logic, it can't be safe. In fact," I said, warming to my theme, "every building in the country must be unsafe. Even the extension we're putting up now is probably unsafe as there's almost certainly a new regulation coming out that it doesn't comply with. It's the ultimate Catch 22 situation. The only buildings that are safe are the ones that haven't yet been built." He looked a little nonplussed and I felt a bit sorry for him. His job after all was to defend the indefensible.

I mention this simply to show how the regulatory regime has gripped so many areas of public life and how regulations have become ends in themselves, to be accepted unquestioningly. As soon as you start questioning, the edifice - unlike one of their buildings - frequently falls apart. Many regulations seem to have little purpose other than to provide work for successive generations of bureaucrats. And, like a sort of bureaucratic knotweed, to undermine the foundations of small businesses.

For years we have heard objections to "the faceless bureaucrats of Brussels" as though the European Union had invented bureaucracy. Now while not wishing to defend the EU against charges of bureaucracy - it's quite clearly up there with the best of them - there is an implication that, left to our own devices, we British would cut bureaucracy to a minimum. I detail later the impressive achievements of one of the grandmasters of the art, the Post Office. I also reveal the agonies caused by Environmental Health Officers, and the tortuous route our successor had to travel to get his drinks' licence. Perhaps this is the place to relate what we called, somewhat verbosely, the Egg Standardisation Scandal, spawned by the policies of the Ministry of Food and Fisheries which spent hundreds of pounds of taxpayers' money to prevent a local farmer selling five dozen free range eggs a week. There was nothing wrong with the eggs, no trace of salmonella or anything else to get Edwina sizzling like a Madras curry (sorry!), just that they hadn't been standardised. We were selling different sized eggs all at the same price. But this wasn't hidden from the customers; there was no suggestion we were secretly passing off pigeon eggs as ostrich eggs. All the eggs were on display and the customers chose the ones they wanted and went off happily to boil, poach, fry or scramble as the gastronomic mood took them. This wasn't anywhere near good enough for the "Men from the Ministry."

It started when one of our customers shopped us. We're not sure who it was, certainly not one of the people we'd mortally offended as none of them came near enough to see whether we were selling free range eggs or free range buffaloes. But the first time the man from the ministry came, he told us there'd been a complaint. And he wanted the name of our supplier.

Our supplier then had a visit from two different officials and was told that if she wanted to carry on supplying eggs, she had to set up a packing station, a process which involved completing a forty page booklet and making alterations to her farm costing several thousand pounds. "It just doesn't seem worth it," she said in one of the great understatements of the twentieth century, "not for five dozen eggs a week."

Thus a very small element of local trade, which provided her with pin money, gave us an addition to our stock and kept a few people in Poulton happy, was nipped in the bud.

"It may only be five dozen eggs today," I can hear the man from the ministry saying, "It'll be a Eurowide omelette industry tomorrow unless it's stopped. He must have believed this, mustn't he, must have felt he was protecting the public from a scam that was costing the Treasury thousands and putting lives at risk. Otherwise how could he justify an operation involving three trips from London by three officials with salaries and expenses amounting to, well, enough to set up a packing station. And this wasn't an outbreak of BSE, E-Coli, or even salmonella. Neither was it a village shopkeeper putting his customers at risk by unhygienic practices. This was a teeny weeny business doing absolutely no harm and a little bit of good, which had a gross turnover of around £300 a year and which no one in their right mind could possibly object to. And this is perhaps the point. Some of these people haven't been anywhere near their right minds for years.

"Yes we'll strangle this at birth," he must have thought. "Get this little example of food fascism while it's still a corporal in some Viennese dosshouse. This is one Hitler that'll never rise to threaten the world."

Of course he never thought any such thing. Probably never thought beyond the fact that a minor infringement of regulations that were pointless anyway offered him - and his colleagues - the chance to swan it in the Cotswolds at taxpayers' expense. Is it any wonder that officials are held in such contempt and that there is a feeling, expressed increasingly, that government officials have replaced college professors as the aloof, out-of-touch inhabitants of those ivory towers?

We could have got round it by giving the eggs away and asking for voluntary contributions from customers. Then we'd have been within the law (that phrase alone emphasises how unreal this was - we're talking sixty eggs a week remember!) but was it worth it? Why bother to jump through all kinds of bureaucratic hoops, follow legal by-passes through a trail of tangled regulations for a gross profit of £2 a week?

And this is just one example. Multiply it by the number of shops in the country and you get some idea of the potential extent of the bureaucratic problem. It wasn't the only example in Poulton by any means though the others weren't related to the shop. One instance worth mentioning concerned a performance licence for a cultural weekend in the grounds of one of Poulton's larger houses - a Shakespeare play on the Friday followed by a musical soiree on the Saturday. To obtain the licence, two employees of the Cotswold District Council inspected the grounds to make sure they were fireproof and that fire escapes were available. "You wouldn't want anyone trapped in a burning garden now would you sir?" These may not have been the exact words but you get the picture. Having conformed to one absurd ritual, the host assumed the licence would be valid or could be extended to cover the following night's concert. "Oh no," he was informed. "Music comes under entertainment. You'll need a different licence for that!"

I have a theory about all this correctness and over-regulation. It's something to do with being constitutionally incapable of counting our blessings. In more than half a century, we have experienced none of life's mega disasters - no famine, no pestilence, no war. But we can't seem to accept a life free of these problems. Old age, illness, the trials of parenthood, drugs, broken homes etc aren't sufficient. We've had to create other demons. So the real fear of polio and TB has been replaced by the fringe worry of food poisoning. The real worry of being bombed by Nazi warplanes or scorched in a nuclear holocaust has been replaced by the fringe worry of tenants being burnt to death by unscrupulous landlords. Victorian mill owners have been replaced by wanton shopkeepers prepared to risk the health of the whole neighbourhood rather than jettison one out-of-date pie. It's not that we shouldn't be concerned about these things, it's just that we seem to have them completely out of proportion.

But at a local level surely bureaucracy is unknown and common sense prevails? Well..er...no actually. Never mind the over-regulation of Brussels, the humourless bureaucrats of Whitehall, the unfathomable workings of the local council, what about Poulton? In a village of around 300 people we have, at a quick count, ten committees with around five members on each. That's right, one committee member for every six residents. And I defy any resident of Poulton to name, with certainty, ten of these people and the committees they sit on. I even defy them to name the committees. Never mind the faceless bureaucrats of Whitehall. What about the faceless bureaucrats of Poulton?

On a lighter note, we'll get back to the house in Swansea that we let to students. At the end of the eminently sensible process of ensuring the house is fireproof, we were required to put up three notices - "To Fire Exit," an arrow, and "Fire Exit" in big green letters over the front door. The house is two storeys and only a complete idiot - like a fire officer? - would try to get out through any exit other than the front door - or the kitchen door if he were in the kitchen. We misplaced the "Fire Exit" notice and had to buy another. On our first visit to the house after the students had moved in, we saw the students had found the missing notice and there were the big green letters on the inside of the toilet seat! Nice to know in this bureaucratic world that some people still have a sense of humour.

Speaking of a sense of humour brings us nicely to another temple of bureaucracy, the Environmental Health Department because no environmental health officer has been known to have one. During an inspection even my best one-liners would be greeted with stonefaced silence. One day at breakfast, Lizzie, scanning the TV programmes, remarked that the next episode of *The Frost Report* concerned the murder of an Environmental Health Officer. I said although there'd be no shortage of suspects, if there was a small shopkeeper in the plot, he would almost certainly be the killer. He might even give himself up in a sort of "hero of the resistance" gesture and receive a free pardon.

In fairness, the trepidation induced in small shopkeepers by Environmental Health Officers is caused by the attitude of just a few of them. Most EHO's are perfectly reasonable and retain a sense of proportion in their implementation of the increasingly stringent regulations coming out of Whitehall. They apply the common sense concept of 'reasonable degree of risk', accepting the idea that there's no such thing as a totally safe food. But a few stalk their patch, stern-faced, gimlet-eyed, looking for something they know is there if only they're sharp enough to find it. And if it isn't, they'll invoke some law condemning something they *have* found. Fridges that are running at slightly less than the requisite level of efficiency, out-of-date washing powder - well it hasn't yet come to that but who knows what new absurdities are lurking just round the corner. And after an inspection by one of the more zealous officers and on the basis of half a dozen minor infringements of regulations, another shopkeeper is journeying to the outer regions of sanity and contemplating closure or suicide. One officer tried consistently to get us to remove the flagstone floor of our shop regardless of the fact that it had been there since the shop originally opened and was one of the features that gave the shop its traditional flavour.

In the face of all logic, we now have sell-by dates on pet food. Given half a chance, dogs and cats will quite happily and with few ill effects scavenge in rubbish and eat maggot-ridden meat, two-week-old chicken bones and any other little chunks of horror they can sink their teeth into yet if the local shopkeeper sells their owners one tin of Chappie that is a day past its sell-by date, and is caught doing it, he faces prosecution and a crippling fine.

I'll mention just one other instance of the "logic" that confronts the small shopkeeper and the crosses he has to bear in his dealings with the Foods Standards Authority. Recorded instances of food poisoning have increased during the last fifteen years and the Environmental Health Department suggests that conditions in small shops and local butchers are probably responsible. Now one thing is certain. Any increase in food poisoning has nothing to do with village shops - or any other small retailers. During the last fifteen years, the number of small food and meat retailers has fallen dramatically while the number of superstores has increased in more or less the same ratio. Any increase in cases of food poisoning is far more likely to be the result of inadequate care taken with chilled meals and other fast food items purchased from supermarkets and elsewhere than a lack of hygiene on the part of small retailers. Poulton Village Stores has been selling food since its opening way back in the mists of time and as far as we know - and certainly for the duration of our tenure - there has never been an instance of food poisoning in Poulton even though the shop sells pies, dairy products and eggs, as well as fresh, chilled and frozen meat.

Perhaps instead of making illogical assertions, officials should establish the instances of food poisoning that can be traced back to small shops. My guess is that they would be very few. Small shopkeepers aren't fools (well I know they became shopkeepers in the first place but that's a different kind of foolishness). They understand the rules of hygiene and the commercial consequences of ignoring them. If an outbreak of food poisoning had occurred in Poulton and been traced to the shop, our customers would have voted with their purses. We'd have gone bankrupt long before the Department of the Environment could have put up the closure signs.

As Tom Boyd notes in *A World in a Grain of Sand*, in the 1930's Albert Edwards, who ran Poulton General Store and stocked just about everything, kept his provisions under his bed next to the chamber pot, a practice that would today warrant immediate closure by the EHO's. In fact, had they been subjected to today's stringent regulations, closure would probably have been the fate of all village food shops of the time yet all their customers, having survived infant diseases, seemed to live to a ripe old age.

Cigarettes will, on all available evidence, cause substantially more damage than yoghurt that is past its sell-by date. Take your pick - a mild case of diarrhoea, or lung cancer. Yet selling one of these items could result in a crippling fine - and it isn't cigarettes. Does no one have the occasional flicker that our priorities no less than our reactions are all wrong?

The EHO's don't need to tell us to keep our stock fresh; the customers will beat them to it. Our small band of loyalists would have shrunk even further if we'd gained a reputation for selling sub-standard products. And, like many other things, it comes down to a question of choice. Some customers regarded sell-by dates as an unacceptable intrusion; others lived and breathed them. But given the standards of quality established by supermarkets, it makes no sense at all for a shopkeeper to keep out-of-date stock on his shelves. When we ran the shop I lived on out-of-date stock and was often referred to as "Out-of-date Stu" (I *think* it referred to what I ate), and in Khartoum, I ate butter that was past its sell-by date even before it reached the shops. And lived to tell the tale. If I was granted a number of wishes, one might be to parachute an Environmental Health Officer into Khartoum market, or the kitchen at the Sudan Club, and watch the citadels of his bureaucracy crumble. He would see carcasses alive with flies and six-month-old yoghurt curdling in warm fridges. He would see waiters coughing and hawking over badly cooked food, and rats in every kitchen. And he would see the street kids eking out a scavenging life with the cats and dogs among the overflowing rubbish skips. All his training, all his regulations would tell him that life in such an environment is impossible. This is the jungle, the bacterial back streets. Surely life can't exist here.

Now I would be the last to suggest that we live our lives according to the standards of Khartoum but thinking of such places might help us get our own regulations into some kind of perspective. Khartoum is at war - against famine, against poverty, against its own people, against *real* disease. It has no time for the niceties of the Environmental Health regime. Only a country with little threat to its well-being can afford the luxury of sell-by dates on tins of pet food. In Khartoum, an EHO would perhaps see his more trivial pre-occupations for what they are - a monumental irrelevance among the greater issues of life, and on his return, have a better sense of proportion about yoghurt that is two days out of date, or bread that is exposed to the public, or synthetic cream in cakes that aren't refrigerated and so on. It certainly needs something dramatic to breach the bureaucratic monolith that is the modern Environmental Health Department.

Our only real environmental concern while we ran the shop was the occasional invasion of mice. Living in countryside backing on to a village shop, the field mice couldn't believe their luck and in the winter made frequent and destructive raids on our stock. We wouldn't have minded if they'd been satisfied with one chocolate bar or one bag of flour. Unfortunately they had a compulsion to sample every item so that in a box of Kit-Kat, for example, each bar would have one corner nibbled away. The mice were one of the reasons we acquired a cat although as they spent a lot of their time scurrying behind the boarding that lined the walls of the living room, the cat, much to his frustration, couldn't get near them. We made several other attempts to control them with varying degrees of success. The electronic rodent repellent, "guaranteed" to remove all manner of pests, was a complete waste of money. Getting the Council Pest Control Unit to lay poison was more successful - although the smell of rotting carcasses permeated the house for weeks. Occasionally, we decided the cat had to earn his keep and put him in the shop overnight. We weren't sure how much of a deterrent it was to the mice but at least it justified us putting all expenses relating to the cat through the books. The VAT man was quite amused to see a vet bill classified as "rodent operative." "I'll allow you that for pure cheek," he commented. The dog was down under the heading "guard dog" - which slightly overstated his usefulness. He terrorised friends and customers yet when the armed robbers were creating mayhem in the shop, he was as quiet as....well, a mouse.

And the mice, apart from the occasional scuttling behind the skirting boards, were usually very quiet indeed. And shy. We saw the results of their stock vandalism yet hardly ever saw a mouse.

The exception was one that hopped into the shop one day when one of our more tenderhearted customers was waiting at the post office.

"Ooh look at the little mouse," she cried as it appeared from behind the counter in full view of a shop full of people. "Ooh look everybody. Isn't he *sweet?*"

Thankfully there wasn't an Environmental Health Officer around at the time. It's unlikely that he would have seen the funny side or described the little pest that had designs on our stock and livelihood as "sweet". But the mice were generally timid souls and kept themselves well-hidden when an Environmental Health Officer was in the vicinity. We were grateful for this and often wished we could have taken the same course of action.

CHAPTER NINE.

CONFLICTS OF INTEREST

.... with a little help from our friends. (**Lennon and McCartney**)

Owe a hundred pounds, you're a failure, owe a thousand pounds you're a businessman, owe a million pounds you're a government, so I think I'm on the way up. (**Andy Capp**)

Several years ago when we were arranging the mortgage to buy the post office, we took the advice of Barclays' Insurance Services and arranged a pension mortgage which, at redemption, we were told would include a lump sum of £36,000 to pay back the capital. In 1994, we switched the mortgage to the Midland Bank who asked for an evaluation of the policy. We found to our alarm that the endowment element was now worth only £25,000 and we had to incur the expense of setting up a repayment mortgage of £11,000. When we had set up the policy, no one had told us that the £36,000 wasn't guaranteed and we had continued blithely on our way, £11,000 worse off than we thought we were.

Banks frequently engage in what can only be termed sharp practice. The experience with our mortgage probably doesn't qualify - although it comes pretty close - but I'm not sure how else to describe some of our other experiences down the years. For example, We have a standing order for our mortgage payments. In 1998, these payments rose in conjunction with interest rates. I forgot to adjust the standing order and the inevitable happened - one month we were overdrawn to the sum of seventeen pence (that's right, seventeen pence). On our next statement I spotted a £25 penalty charge and, on inquiry, was told that this was the standard charge for an unauthorised overdraft.

Twenty-five pounds for going seventeen pence overdrawn. I registered my displeasure in no uncertain terms. The bank apologised and withdrew the charge but the point was why it was imposed in the first place. One of the ritual excuses is that it's the computer's fault. But computers are programmed. They don't suddenly take it into their own heads to take £25 from Mr and Mrs

Russell's account and the fact that they're programmed to do so can only be called stealthy financing. Or sharp practice. They rely on the fact that the majority of customers won't spot such sur-charges or if they do will assume the bank is within its rights and there's nothing they can do about it.

The problem if you're dissatisfied with your bank (as people, sooner or later invariably are) is that you can't go to any of the other banks and expect better treatment - at least not after the introductory serenades and overtures. I was outraged but not surprised by a recent TV programme exposing the "inefficiency" of the banks in grossly overcharging some of their customers. The most interesting point made during the programme was that computers were programmed to guard against undercharging, but not against overcharging. So much for the myth of "It's the com-puter's fault." Friends of ours had great difficulty extending their mortgage by £10,000 yet independently were offered a personal loan by the same bank of up to £15,000 to spend as they wished. The rate of interest on the loan was of course almost double that on the mortgage. Surely there couldn't be any connection between the offer of a loan and their application for a mortgage? Or have I just got a suspicious mind?

Businesses, particularly small businesses, operate in spite of banks. I've already described how much our bank manager cost us by recommending the wrong accountant. Bank charges are loaded against them and there is always a substantial fee for arranging an overdraft (see below.) And when you *really* need their help, they turn the other way. It's the financial equivalent of Catch 22. "We'll only help you if you don't need our help. If you do need it, we won't help you." Some catch! My stepson after completing his degree and before starting his barrister's course at Lincoln's Inn, went on a scholarship to Japan. Before leaving, he'd arranged a £1000 overdraft with his bank. Or thought he had. When he wrote a cheque from Japan for the deposit on his bar school course, it was 'returned to drawer' as there were no funds to cover it. Luckily we were on hand to phone Lincoln's Inn, explain the mistake and honour the cheque. A promising legal career might have been nipped in the bud through the inefficiency of the bank both in failing to record the overdraft agreement and in dishonouring what was obviously a fairly important cheque without even mak-ing a few phone calls. They did at least acknowledge their mistake and gave him £50 in compensation. My God, these banks know how to atone for their sins. £50 for risking a whole career elo-quently expresses what I'm trying to say.

When the bank manager wanted to speak to me it was usually about our overdraft. I never understood why. It never went above three thousand pounds and there was always significantly more on deposit to cover it. Yet periodically I would receive phone calls, which always began: "We're a little worried about your overdraft."

Always the collective "we" as if the length and size of our overdraft were the subjects of interminable mutterings and speculation along the corridors of high finance until a consensus was reached that something had to be done about it.

"Up it to £30,000 - then they'll respect you," a well-wisher said one day. I wasn't worried about our overdraft. Why should they be, except, as I later realised, as a means of wheedling more money out of us, putting a few more straws on the overburdened backs of a pair of village shopkeepers.

"Why?" I wanted to say. "You have ten thousand businessmen cashing cheques, owing you money, negotiating loans. You have pension schemes, mortgage arrangements, personal equity plans, TESSAS, equities, offshore trusts, and four or five kinds of interest bearing account. You have branches in a hundred countries scattered across the globe. You have sufficient financial interest to see you through the next millennium, let alone this one. So why this regular compulsion to discuss my overdraft? A bit like me phoning Mrs. Jones to tell her she still hasn't paid for the box of matches I let her have two days ago. Or the small boy who suddenly remembers he hasn't teased the cat for a week or two and spends the afternoon driving the poor moggy to distraction. This compulsion to discuss my overdraft was Chinese torture.

"Have you thought about converting it to a business loan?"

"Think about little else," I want to reply. "In those twilight hours when I'm drifting off to sleep and a myriad thoughts flit through my head, that's the one that keeps recurring. "Should I convert my overdraft to a business loan?"

"Er...no. I'd just like to renew my overdraft."

"Can't do that as easily now." Somebody higher up has obviously ordered him to convert all overdrafts to business loans. "You'll have to pay a new setting up charge."

"Seventy five pounds?"

"A hundred," he says and adds in explanation. "Inflation."

"Inflation at thirty three percent?" I almost ask, but let it go. It's a no-win situation.

"You really should think about a business loan," he says and I get the feeling I'm to be given little choice in the matter. He explains the terms; I know the business can't satisfy them. There's no way short of robbing a bank (now, there's an idea) that I shall ever pay off a loan with interest charges of 12% in two years. And he should know it too, unless he's a financial illiterate. (Which, come to think of it....)

"I'll pay it off," I suddenly blurt out.

"Good man," he says introducing the patronising tone into his voice that always makes me want to strangle him. "I knew you'd see sense."

"The overdraft. I'll pay it off."

"With a business loan?"

"With cash."

That's stumped him.

"Cash?"

"From my select account."

"Oh. Are you happy about that?

"Over the moon," I say, suddenly released from the curse of the overdraft. So we settle it. He arranges to transfer the funds, I say I hope he has a nice day.

"Now," I say as our transaction draws to a close. "I'd still like a little overdraft - just to cover the odd cheque."

"There's no such thing as a little overdraft," he says "Not administratively."

"Three hundred pounds," I inquire hopefully. "Is that little?"

I can feel him shaking his head. "I'll still have to charge you for setting it up."

"How much?" I ask but I already know. "A hundred pounds."

"Why?" I ask as though our interchange has been based on anything approaching reason.

"Well, there's computer records to change."

"Two minutes work."

"Then I've got to make sure the money's available."

Now I'm really astonished. "That   is Barclays Bank I'm talking to, isn't it?"

"Pardon."

"I thought for a minute I'd got in touch with the local charity shop. You mean to tell me that this multinational billions-of-profits-per-annum organisation that I and millions of others trust with their financial lives cannot guarantee to have three hundred pounds available at a second's notice. Forget it. I know a couple of pensioners who'll lend me the money. I'm not sure my money's safe with you. I think I'll switch everything to the Midland."

"Three hundred pounds" he says tonelessly and puts the phone down.

The smugness that drifts down the line when he knows he's got the better of me has gone. For once I feel *I've* got the better of *him*. I also know I've got the better of him and his cronies in another way. I've been using our personal account for business transactions for two or three years now. I've thwarted their attempts to bankrupt us with bank charges. Now I've nipped in the bud their attempt to bankrupt us with interest on a business loan.

So of the three financial services we needed to run our business -

accountants, banking, and insurance - we had spent a lot of money discovering the unsuitability of one, and we were aware – though we could do little about it - of the unreliability of another. But the third, insurance services, we somehow regarded as beyond reproach, peopled by agents and brokers who had our best interests firmly in their hearts. Two or three times over the previous few years, I'd discovered this was way short of the truth. It is the attitude of the insurance companies that is responsible for clients' practice of loading claims and getting traders to mark up invoices to cover the compulsory excess. Insurance is a battlefield where the companies try to pay as little compensation as possible and the claimants push the claims as high as they dare.

When our car was stolen, we had to wait six weeks before it was officially declared non-recoverable - by the insurance company, of course, not by us or even by the police - and they coughed up the cash for a replacement. Six weeks during which, without the loan of a car from friends, we would either have been without a car or had to hire one at our own expense. In addition we lost our no claims bonus over something that was demonstrably not our fault. We had taken out the policy in good faith. And we did indeed get another vehicle out of it - but no one had told us about the six weeks' waiting time. Six weeks is a long time for a business to be without transport and for a family to be stranded in a Cotswold village at the mercy of the rural bus service.

For three or four years, I had been paying nearly six hundred pounds a year for a property and business insurance through a particular broker. Every year the broker told me that he had failed to locate a cheaper deal and recommended I carry on as before, a recommendation I took completely on trust. However, one year just before my premium was due, I received a call from another firm who after being given details of the cover I wanted, informed me that they could offer me the same insurance for three hundred and twenty pounds. I immediately phoned my broker and informed him that I had received a better offer which I had until the following day to accept. The same afternoon he phoned back saying he'd discovered a means by which he could now reduce my premium to just over three hundred pounds.

He couldn't understand why I reacted so angrily, not even when I explained that his deceit or incompetence had cost me almost a thousand pounds over the previous three years. Ultimately, after I'd calmed down, I realised that the blame lay fairly and squarely with me. I should have shopped around years ago, playing one company off against another. I had something they wanted and I should have negotiated the best terms for me. I couldn't really expect them to do it. After all, no other company is in business for *your* benefit. We learned this to our cost. I used to think that banks and insurance companies had the same ethical standards as schools and hospitals. But any health or educational institution which treated patients or students like our bank, our first accountant and our insurance broker treated us would face regular and crippling prosecutions. We learned the hard way and eventually changed our accountant and our insurance broker. But there was little point in changing our bank. The main banks all sing from the same hymn sheet and operate what is in all but name a cartel. And there seems little that anyone in authority is prepared to do about it.

CHAPTER SIX

THE DAILY PAPER CHASE

Ladies and gentlemen, I give you the most inefficient wholesaling organisation in the history of the known universe. W.H. Smith of Gloucester created more pressure than Banks and Environmental Health Officers put together. Maybe it wasn't quite such worrying pressure - after all W.H. Smith never threatened us with closure or bankruptcy, just insanity. And there was nothing vindictive or even self-seeking about it, just plain inefficiency. Almost every day they got my order wrong and it was often impossible to contact them. "So why didn't you change them?" I can hear someone asking. And you might well ask, as it seems the logical course of action. Let me explain.

We were delighted when we took over the newspapers and pleased to have the whole range to scan during the day although we disapproved of the attitudes and pre-occupations of some of the tabloids, the so-called "red-tops". If I could have chosen, I perhaps wouldn't have stocked the *Sun*. The vilification of such patently nice men as Neil Kinnock and Graham Taylor goes way beyond questions of public interest, as does the coverage of lesser people's private lives. It was significant that on the day the Irish peace agreement was signed the *Sun* relegated it to Page 5, the first three pages dealing exclusively with George Michael's act of self abuse in a public toilet. Was this reflecting the priorities of its readers or attempting to shape them in its own image? Sheridan's line in *School for Scandal*, "They murder characters to kill time", could have been written with the tabloids in mind. So if I could have chosen, the *Sun* may not have been included in our daily order. But the key phrase is "if I could have chosen". In the case of groceries, greeting cards, fruit and vegetables, bread, shoelaces, batteries, copper reliefs, even Christmas wine and fresh fish we could choose both the product and the supplier.

Not with newspapers. We were told both who our supplier would be and what newspapers we could sell. So however inefficient our wholesalers W.H. Smith were - and believe me they turned inefficiency into an art form - we couldn't change them. Our newspaper wholesalers were determined by - well, by newspaper wholesalers. The newspaper wholesaling business is in effect a cartel and its operation goes directly counter to the alleged policies of successive governments of encouraging efficiency through competition. The only way to have ceased trading with W.H. Smith was to have stopped selling newspapers altogether. In this age of increased competition, of greater choice, of greater freedom in the market place, retail newsagents cannot choose their wholesaler. News distributors have as big a monopoly as the water companies. And unlike the water companies, there is no Offwat to ensure they exercise restraint. The equivalent of Offwat should be the Federation of Retail Newsagents but sadly it appears to be as useful as the proverbial chocolate teapot. If ever there was a case for concerted action it is by all the newsagents in the land to break the cartel operated by the wholesalers.

None of this concerned us when we started selling newspapers. Our supplier then was MS Group of Swindon and they proved thoroughly satisfactory. After a few years, we were suddenly informed that our wholesaler for some titles was being changed. From now on Mirror Group Newspapers would be delivered by W.H. Smith of Gloucester. At the time the change involved only the *Daily Mirror* and *The European*. Our daily order for *Mirrors* was ten, our weekly order for *The European* was one. Every day a van had to come from Gloucester to Poulton to drop off ten *Mirrors*. It involved us in two separate orders, two separate returns, and, more importantly, two delivery charges. I spoke to the Federation of Retail Newsagents who said they could do nothing. I then had a chat to the W.H. Smith manager and the MS Group manager and we agreed that it made sense for MS to supply the *Mirrors* with the rest of the order. They were prepared to sanction this *providing we all kept quiet about it.* It was reassuring for once to see common sense prevailing - it's amazing in the modern world how frequently common sense *doesn't* prevail - but we found the clandestine nature of the operation quite astonishing. We were talking about a trading arrangement that involved 61 items a week at a few pence per item and behaving like people selling state secrets to the Russians.

About two years later, again without warning, I was informed that *all* our supplies would be delivered by W.H. Smith. It made more sense than delivering only ten *Mirrors*, but not much more. I was perfectly happy with MS Group, and their depot in Swindon is about half the distance to Gloucester. Again I contacted the Federation. Again they told me they could do nothing.

So there we were, stuck with a change of wholesaler we hadn't asked for and could do nothing about. To compound the situation, it soon became clear that whereas MS Group had proved thoroughly efficient, W.H. Smith were their "mirror image" (pardon the pun), often making more mistakes in a week than MS Group had made in five years. They also developed the infuriating habit of adjusting supplies without warning so that on any day and for any title, not only were we without spare copies, we sometimes didn't have enough to meet regular orders. No amount of telephone calls and letters could effect a permanent change.

One of the many problems with W.H. Smith was their insistence on "boxing out", that is sending us copies of magazines that we hadn't ordered. Such magazines were supplied on a sale-or-return basis but with our limited shelf space we found them difficult to display, rarely sold them and occasionally forgot to send them back. This practice might work with the larger newsagents but for a village shop with a limited clientele it is a waste of time. And space. I explained this frequently to the wholesalers but although they said they understood the problem, they continued to box out titles irrespective of requests or the nature of the establishment.

Some of the boxings out, to put it delicately, showed a lack of common sense. There are magazines that cater for all tastes and hobbies and our regular orders reflected this. We supplied copies of such magazines as *Speedway Mail, Cycling, Dog World, Antique Clocks*, and *Gibbons Stamp Monthly* to name a few - and what a wonderful diversity of human interests was reflected in the magazine orders even from a shop as small as ours. These magazines were ordered specifically by customers with those particular interests and were hardly likely to be bought by an uninterested shopper. One of the boxings out was a magazine called *Practical Fishkeeping*. Hardly the magazine for a casual purchaser, not exactly an impulse buy. Nobody browsing round our shelves was likely to see the magazine and think, "Just what I need. I'll start to keep fish." Again although we had a regular order for one copy of *Gibbons Stamp Monthly* there was no logical reason for sending the two that frequently came, as though stamp collectors can be conjured up to match the magazine order rather than the other way round.

I sometimes received copies of what are euphemistically called 'Men's Magazines' or 'General Entertainment' and occasionally, when I was sorting out my *Independents* and *Telegraphs* in the morning, the picture of a naked woman would confront me. (No, this *wasn't* the reason mistakes were sometimes made in the rounds - I wasn't sent these magazines *that* often). I pointed out to W.H. Smith that we ran a small shop with a number of elderly customers of conservative tastes who would have been shocked to find such magazines on our shelves. Others would have seen them as changing the ambience of the shop and introducing an element of bad taste. Whether such magazines have a place elsewhere I leave others to judge. But we felt they had no place in an establishment as intimate and innately conservative as a village stores. But, irrespective of our views, the magazines kept coming and I kept sending them back.

So newspapers from being the smoothest aspect of the business became fraught with problems, not the least of which being W.H. Smith's aversion to answering the phone. Running a shop means that phone calls have to be squeezed in during quiet periods yet no quiet period was long enough for the W.H. Smith telephone girls. One morning I left the phone ringing while I served several customers. It was still ringing twenty minutes later and I gave up. When I eventually got through I was told that it was too late to be credited for deficiencies in that morning's order and I should have reported them earlier. Have *you* ever felt like spitting into a phone?

And although efforts were made to put the blame on one aspect of the business, experience showed that inefficiency was rife throughout the organisation. Sometimes it was the fault of the girl who took the order - the documents would show that she'd copied it down wrongly. Sometimes the packers had only packed fifteen *Daily Mails* instead of eighteen ("Some of our packers can't count" the manager would say, as though this absolved him of all responsibility). And sometimes it was the drivers who had delivered a bundle to the wrong place – the drivers shared the brunt of the criticism with those universal scapegoats, the computers.

"Please can you make sure I have eight *Expresses* every day for the foreseeable future?" I would plead on one of the rare occasions I managed to get through.

I would be suitably reassured. The trouble was that W.H. Smith were notoriously short-sighted and the foreseeable future stretched only to the following week.

"It's the computer's fault" the girl would say when I finally got through to her and asked why my *Expresses* had plummeted to five. "They're programmed and we can do nothing about it."

"You should work in a bank," I said and put the phone down.

Recently they introduced a system of sending magazines in grey boxes. Each box would probably take twenty magazines. The other morning, while running the business for Rob and Sue, I received three different titles delivered - you've probably guessed - in three different boxes, each box containing one or two magazines. I put the boxes out to be collected the next morning but they weren't. Neither were they collected the morning after. Grey boxes were piling up in an establishment where storage space was at a premium. They couldn't be thrown away as there is a charge of £10 for every box missing. The whole saga was vintage W.H. Smith.

So W.H. Smith were (and I understand still are) a disaster, the cartel an affront to all ethical business practice and the Federation utterly anaemic. When our baker, greengrocer, grocery suppliers, yoghurt makers, milk wholesaler, greeting card distributors, pie manufacturers, etc sent us unordered and unwanted products, we sent them back and received full credit. If any of them had behaved like W.H. Smith, we would have looked for a new supplier. The fact that we couldn't do this with the newspapers simply emphasised the lack of commercial freedom in the newspaper business.

CHAPTER TEN.

DAYLIGHT ROBBERY

We had two instances of robbery during our tenure of Poulton post office. The first was when a few drunken louts broke two of our windows to steal chocolate for their girl friends the night before we were setting off for a weekend in Amsterdam. In the early hours of the morning I was cutting and nailing plywood to the broken windows while the police, complete with tracker dog, followed a trail of Cadbury's cream eggs deep into the Gloucestershire countryside.

The other was altogether more serious. Three days before Christmas 1992, the post office was robbed at gunpoint. The experience is etched on my memory: time 11.50 a.m. day: Tuesday: date 22nd December. Lizzie at the cash and carry. Me alone in the shop.

The recollection is blurred and impressionistic. One minute I was engaged in a low-key activity (sticking stamps on Christmas cards), the next I was lying face down with a gun in my back, one squeeze of an index finger away from serious injury. In the intervening period, three figures in balaclavas had burst into the shop, two with shotguns, the other brandishing a stick. At first I thought it was my son and his friends playing a practical joke, realising immediately that it wasn't. I had been threatened with guns before - in Zambia at a sensitive border post, in Khartoum when I had unwittingly broken the curfew - without feeling anything like as vulnerable as when these marauding strangers invaded my own premises. Some instinct told me to remove my glasses and place them on a nearby shelf while, behind me, mayhem was taking place. One of them swore as he inadvertently closed the post office door and speaking more calmly than I felt, I offered them the keys. They ignored me and smashed the anti-bandit screen - so much for the protection offered by Post Office hardware. An interminable time seemed to pass during which I anticipated at best a blow on the head until suddenly I realised they were leaving. The last one touched me on the shoulder, a strangely comforting gesture from a person who, with his colleagues, had created such a watershed in my life. The shop door slammed and as the car roared away I got to my feet. The incident, which changed our lives and perceptions, lasted all of four minutes. The hand on the shoulder had said "Relax. It's over."

And I thought it was. My over-riding feeling was one of relief - as intense as anything I have ever felt. I rushed to the door and got a description of the car - a white sports model. I couldn't get the number or the make but questioned their intelligence in using a car that was so eye-catching. (It was later found abandoned - they'd switched cars a few miles from the shop.)

I then went to phone the police. My stepdaughter was speaking on the upstairs extension - probably discussing her social life with one of her school friends, I thought, but she wasn't. She was reporting the robbery. She'd heard the noise and thought at first that it was "Stuart having a row with a customer." Ignoring what this says about her perception of my customer relations, I was impressed by her presence of mind. She must have realised that none of my rows - have I ever had any rows? - involved breaking glass and she had sneaked a look in the shop. Seeing what was happening, she phoned the police.

Lying behind the counter many fears rushed through my mind - that I would be shot, that the robbers would ransack the house, that a customer would come in and the thieves would panic. This was one occasion when I definitely did *not* want customers. Indeed, from one point of view, the incident is another indictment of the support given to village shops that at midday, on the Tuesday before Christmas, armed robbers could attack the post office without being disturbed.

After the police had been contacted, I informed the Post Office who arranged to send auditors and inspectors. Then the phone started ringing. First it was Radio Gloucester asking me to make a statement. I refused, but was amazed at their speed off the mark. Next the local newspaper phoned wanting to send a reporter round. I told them to contact the Post Office Publicity Department in Bristol. By the time GWR, the Wiltshire radio station, phoned, my resistance had weakened. I answered their questions and, I believe, made a general statement about the robbery. Within seconds there was a phone call from my daughter who had heard me speaking on GWR. Puzzlement gave way to anger as I realised that my interview had been broadcast live. In their desire to get news almost as it happened, they had violated my privacy a second time. To this day I have no idea what their questions were or whether anything I said was an accurate representation of either the situation or my attitude and responses. They had caught me with my guard down and my mind in chaos, and had given me a taste of media intrusion, an inkling of what it must be like to have tabloid journalists camping on your doorstep and tearing your privacy to shreds.

After the robbery, for the first time we asked ourselves questions about the nature of the job we'd taken on and wondered why anybody becomes a subpostmaster. It certainly isn't for the money. We receive modest remuneration (in many cases "modest" is an overstatement). The average pay of a village subpostmaster is well below the national average although the organisation he works for consistently makes a healthy profit. Subpostmasters work at least one evening every week without pay when they are required by the terms of their contract to complete the weekly accounts. We have to understand numerous types of transaction, learn new business, always present a friendly face, take the responsibility - and the danger - of looking after thousands of pounds worth of stock and cash which makes us among the most vulnerable of businesses - criminals *know* post offices have money - receive no 'danger money', scant protection, no compensation if anything happens and often for a salary which no self-respecting labourer would tolerate.

I say no compensation. Our visiting officer gave us a twenty-pound Threshers' voucher. We took it as an insult until we learned that he'd done it out of the goodness of his own heart - and probably his own pocket. There is no Post Office fund or indeed policy on such matters as robberies, or apparently on much else to do with personnel. When we retired, our Retail Network Manager took us out to lunch but again only because she wanted to. We had served the Post Office and the village well (we think) for over twelve years but had she not decided to treat us to lunch, we would have left without any acknowledgement at all.

The Post Office personnel who came to investigate the robbery - we were still under the auspices of Gloucester - were very sympathetic. Even the auditor, a bespectacled hawkeye of a woman who I had earlier earmarked as "out to get me", was the soul of moderation, accepting my version of events and carrying out the audit accordingly. Only the following day when I was interviewed by the officer from the Post Office Security Service (known to his intimates as the "rottweiler") did I detect a lack of sympathy. He acted as though I was the accused rather than the victim and I felt threatened all over again. I learned later that Head Office in South Wales had suggested that I was somehow to blame for the robbery and raised the possibility of claiming compensation for the lost cash and stock. The security man who I had thought so hostile defended me, maintaining that "no blame whatsoever could be attached to Mr Russell." So much for my judgement of people. The rottweiler turned out to be a nice family pet.

As it happened, the thieves would have escaped with no cash at all if, that morning, I hadn't made a loan to the post office. Just prior to the robbery, our weekly cash delivery had been taken over by a Post Office security firm called Cashco. Previously it had been

146

delivered with the ordinary mail. As with all changes involving the Post Office, it didn't go smoothly and we were frequently in a state of "Will it or won't it?" on the day the money was due. I preferred the old system when I used to track down the postman's van and help myself to the cash (although now I think of it, it was probably such practices that caused the system to be changed in the first place.) The delivery on the day of the robbery had been postponed until the Wednesday and we were desperately low on funds. The previous day I'd drawn two thousand pounds from the bank to settle a few debts and to finance Christmas and, to tide us over the crisis, I decided to lend this money to the post office. (In passing, I should point out that lending money to the Post Office is something postmasters do from time to time and the Post Office is quite relaxed about it. There is even a place in the cash account for "Loan to the Post Office". *BUT* - if a postmaster is caught borrowing the smallest unauthorised amount *from* the Post Office, the high jump awaits. There is no place in the cash account for loan *from* the Post Office.)

So the thieves actually got away with my money. I also expressed regret that I'd actually put the money in the post office in the first place, but the inspectors shook their heads. "The robbers would never have believed you had no cash. They'd have beaten you up before they accepted you were telling the truth." (He could have added that hardworking thieves would have been appalled at such incompetence - both from me and from the Post Office. The least they could expect when they took the trouble to rob a place was to find something there to be stolen).

One of the officials remarked that it was a good job I'd had the presence of mind not to set the alarm off otherwise the robbers might have panicked. I hadn't even had the presence of mind to remember there *was* an alarm but his remark set me thinking. Whenever the alarm had gone off, either in the house or the post office, it had always been by accident. The only effect our alarm systems ever had was to frighten customers out of their wits, to tell Lizzie that I'd locked myself in the post office, to cause squads of police cars to descend on Poulton in the middle of the night on an abortive mission, and to cause Joyce Tucker to abandon her ablutions and rush to the aid of Barbara McIntyre when we were on holiday. Then, on the one occasion the system might have come into its own, I was congratulated for *not* using it. Don't these things occasionally make you wonder?

The trauma from the robbery lasted several months. It affected my work and my leisure and intensified my long-standing claustrophobia. For a long time I couldn't face any social activities and it was February 14th - almost two months later - before I ventured out, to a Valentine Day's lunch in Cheltenham and felt relaxed enough to enjoy it. I inquired about compensation but was told that I wasn't eligible as I had suffered no injury. Injury to the nervous system apparently doesn't count.

I became erratic in my dealings with customers and found it difficult to control my reactions when I thought I was being taken advantage of. One woman who particularly suffered was Rose Savey, the "sherry" woman mentioned in a previous chapter. Unhappily for Rose, she came in the day after the robbery and asked for extra credit. I cursed her roundly and called Lizzie to serve her. For the next few weeks, whenever Rose appeared, I dashed out like a scalded cat yelling "LIZZIE!" Eventually, and understandably, Den and Rose decided to take their custom elsewhere. Not for the first time, they left. And not for the first time they came back. I explained that it was nothing against Rose personally, just a reflex reaction every time I saw her. It must have done wonders for the poor woman's self-confidence.

Thinking back on the extent of the trauma caused by a comparatively minor violation of my territory gave me an increased awareness of the anguish suffered by people who undergo more intense forms of violation. Every time I hear of a rape, a mugging, an instance of grievous bodily harm, a serious road accident, I now have a better idea of what the victim is going through and the thought that throughout the world dictators and their military thugs are allowed to induce such trauma on a massive scale is one of the great international scandals of our time.

A few good things resulted from this unfortunate episode, not least the letters of goodwill and support we received from so many people in Poulton and the surrounding villages. It was the first time that we appreciated how much affection many of our customers felt for us

It was also interesting to hear people's reactions to the robbery. The usual question wasn't "How are you?" - they could see I was superficially all right - but "Have they caught them yet?" I honestly wasn't very interested as to whether they had caught them or not. As a responsible citizen, I suppose I should have wanted them caught to spare other subpostmasters my ordeal, but from a personal point of view it didn't matter much. I felt no anger against those men who in one brief interlude of mayhem had so affected the kilter of our lives. In fact, having shared such a traumatic experience with them - albeit from a different viewpoint - I felt a certain intimacy. I would have liked to sit down with them and talk it over, explaining the effect their actions had had on our lives. Another question a few people asked was "Were they black?" as though this would have made any difference. Some of them probably heard that they were white with mixed feelings. They would no doubt have liked their racial stereotyping confirmed but at the same time felt some disquiet that the "black crimewave" from Bristol and such places was sweeping towards the Cotswolds.

There was also a misunderstanding about our position in the shop. "Aren't you afraid to go back in?" "Weren't you glad that that you were in charge and not Lizzie?" and "Will you ever leave Lizzie on her own in the shop again?" were some of the questions we were asked. I can honestly say we never discussed such matters. I was glad it had happened to me rather than to her in the sense that you'd rather *any* nasty experience happen to you rather than to those you love. But the after effects were in no way rational and the fear, if any, was certainly not the fear of the same thing happening again. In fact, if it *had* happened again, I would have been better prepared. My system, having experienced it once, would have been better able to cope.

Immediately after the robbery, the police couldn't have been more considerate, advising me to be aware of delayed reactions and to consider taking advantage of the Post Office counselling service. I didn't think I needed counselling but a week or so later I changed my mind. I had two or three sessions with the counsellor, a quiet-spoken man who just encouraged me to talk. "You've blown a few fuses." was how he explained my intermittent bouts of anger. " It'll take time for your body to repair the circuits." I also received counselling from the village psychiatrist who told me that the only thing that would make a difference was time. "In four or five months, you'll suddenly realise that you haven't felt the onset of panic or anger for some time now." She was right, although even now, several years later, vestiges of the experience still linger.

A few residents thought that the robbery would mark the end of Poulton Post Office Stores but I can honestly say we were never once tempted either to close or to sell up. I certainly felt shaken and confused but this eventually passed and we soon started looking to the future again and getting our minds back on the serious business of shopkeeping.

PART FIVE

WIDER ISSUES

CHAPTER ONE

COMMUNITY SERVICE

During my time as Poulton's postmaster, I was occasionally invited to give talks to local associations. I usually chose to talk about village shops and their role in maintaining the cohesion of the communities they serve as I thought this was probably the most important subject I was familiar with. (One of the associations was the Hard of Hearing Society and there were the inevitable comments about giving talks to people who couldn't hear. I accepted such comments with my customary grace and forbearance). The next three chapters contain the essence of what I tried to convey.

After a few years running the shop, we raised our sights above the personal level and started to think in terms of village shops generally. We began see our own establishment in the twin contexts of the local community and of village shops throughout the country. We moved from the particular to the general. We had seen the threat to the shop as a threat to us; we began to see it as a threat to the community.

A village community is created by its institutions - the shop, the post office, the church, the pub, the school - and its shared activities - shopping together, drinking together, worshipping together, learning together, doing various things in the village hall together. Some of these institutions exclude certain groups - people who are not practising Christians don't go to church; people without children are not involved with the school; teetotallers don't use the pub. But most people post letters and pay bills at the post office and everybody shops - though sadly not at the village shop.

Of course rural areas haven't degenerated to anything like the extent of their urban counterparts. Poulton retains the sense of community that characterised all habitats fifty years ago. The old framework is still in place but the institutions that support it are dwindling. Poulton used to boast five shops, three pubs, a church, a chapel and a school. Now it has one shop, one pub and the church. It is still a community, but a massive responsibility now rests on these three institutions to provide the necessary cohesion (I should point out that when I refer to the shop, I also include the post office. The two strands of the business are interdependent; one cannot survive without the other. So when the post office loses business the shop is also threatened and vice versa).

There are many advantages in being part of a community. To start with, there's the comfort of never being completely alone. When a personal tragedy occurs, nothing can remotely compensate but if there is someone to talk to, the burden is eased and the loneliness felt by many older people today, when grown up children no longer take up residence in the adjoining street, is relieved. This role of general comforter is partly filled by village shopkeepers and residents often came to us for a consoling chat or a shoulder to cry on when things had gone wrong in their lives.

The shop is the heart of the community. Remove the heart and what's left is a corpse: nothing to give the community life and to pump the communal blood round the village. Village shopkeepers know virtually everyone and are among the first to hear if anything is wrong. Some of the changes affecting rural communities make the survival of the village shop all the more important. The higher costs and reduction in local bus services have made life especially difficult for elderly people and people without cars. As well as providing food and other items, a village shop is a place to meet and exchange information, with a friendly face behind the counter offering personal attention. "When a village loses its shop, it doesn't just lose a convenience, it loses its heart," laments one village whose village shop recently closed. Like many other things, shops are only truly valued when they are no longer there.

Many village shops are under threat because of the soaring value of freeholds. Village shopkeepers are often elderly people living in valuable properties and when the owner decides to retire, the problem of finding a buyer is made more difficult by the value of the freehold. The accounts will rarely support a big enough loan to buy the property and the buyer needs either a partner earning a high salary or a large chunk of capital to invest. What frequently happens is that the shop closes and either the shopkeeper continues to live in the house, or the property is sold as a private dwelling.

We tended to define people in terms of how much they used the shop. Firstly there were the people who genuinely valued it and who supported it even though their personal circumstances didn't necessitate this - they were well off, they had transport, they could - and no doubt did - use the supermarkets as well. Secondly there were the people who used it enough to keep it viable if everybody in the village had used it to the same extent. Of the rest, some popped in occasionally, usually for a paper or a carton of milk. Sometimes they would expose their lack of familiarity with our stock and layout by asking whether we sold a particular item.

Then there were the people who came in every day for their news-paper and never bought anything else, the "one-item" customers as I called them. Others used the post office but not the shop. And finally there were the people who never set foot in the place and who, we must assume, didn't care whether the shop was there or not. Unfortunately, even in Poulton, which seems to value its shop, the majority of residents were in this last category. For them the shop – their shop - was an irrelevance. Until they tried to sell their houses, that is, and found their properties had retained one aspect of their market appeal on the backs of the people who had kept the shop open. (According to a recent report in *The Times*, property prices in villages with shops can be as much as fifteen percent higher than in those without.) Or until they grew old, or sick, or subjected to a petrol blockade, or perhaps until they were ......snowbound.

We love snow. Vestigial feelings of childhood surface when we wake to find the world white, the streets quiet, and the trees and fields looking like a Christmas card. Snow conjures visions of our two daughters, one on a liner sailing along the Alaskan coastline in spring, the other snowboarding in the French Alps. Or perhaps Lizzie and me walking across King Charles's bridge in the roman-tic whiteness of Prague. In the more mundane surroundings of the Cotswolds, snow meant tobogganing in the Coln Valley, and a day significantly different from the rest. Snow is a metaphor for blind optimism. It's always the whiteness and crispness that catches the imagination - not the treachery for drivers and old people, the brown slushiness as the temperature rises, or the ice as the tem-perature falls again and the slush freezes. But at the start it is a day of muffled sounds, strange silences and an absence of traffic. It is also a day when people suddenly appreciate the village shop.

People we hardly knew would appear from nowhere and greet us like long lost friends, which was irritating, or everyday ac-quaintances, which was worse. Some of them had probably needed a map reference to find us. "This is the village shop," we would say finding a little sarcasm irresistible, "You must have taken a wrong turning." Not many of them showed a conscience, or came back when the snow had cleared. Perhaps a few started to appreciate us and made a few vows like a child in trouble. "Get me out of this mess, God, and I promise I'll be good forever." That kind of thing.

But most seemed to think we existed simply for their conven-ience in cases of emergency, a sort of retail equivalent of Live Aid, and that even in this age of punitive sell-by dates, we should have been prepared to stock unlimited supplies just in case a freak snowstorm quadrupled demand. And oh the indignation when we said that we didn't stock a certain item or that we usually stocked it but supplies had run out. Such occasions showed how little people knew about the tribulations of running a shop, the fine balance between cash flow and stock control that made the difference between profit and penury. And why should they have known? It wasn't their line of business. It would have been unreasonable to expect them to know if we hadn't pointed it out a million times. Still, the indignation of village shopkeepers knows no barriers of logic or sense. We just had to express it as good-humoured irony and not as resentment.

When the village and its surrounds were snowbound, our home delivery service came into its own. Like other rural villages, Poulton is surrounded by much sparsely populated countryside which is bleakly isolated during severe weather. Some of the people living in these areas are pensioners with little money and no one to ensure that they're coping. During such times they rely on the local shopkeeper to deliver groceries and particularly coal. One hates to think how they will cope if village shops are consigned to history. Their fate then might well depend on the philanthropy of neighbours which is salutary but not quite as reliable. The village shop is not an individual but an institution. We served these people not as private people but as their local shopkeepers. If we weren't there, somebody else would be as long as the shop existed. If the time comes when it doesn't exist, winters will be even more traumatic for the people who need us.

The heaviest snowfall for years occurred one Saturday just before Christmas when all roads to adjoining towns and villages were blocked. The weight of snow brought down the central feature of our garden, a picturesque but blighted apple tree that sagged and crumpled. When I woke to see snow covering the windows, my first thoughts turned to the paperboys and I wondered how they would cope. One saw the snow as an adventure. He was up even earlier than usual, his footsteps pioneering a way through the whiteness. To the other it was definitely a nuisance but he eventually set off, his deliveries further delayed by the snowball fights he engaged in on the way.

On such occasions, the village was brought together in a kind of comradeship. People enthusiastically fell back on local resources like a kind of rural Swiss Family Robinson, or a wagon train in the wild west closing ranks to stave off a crisis. Within minutes of opening, the shop was full. People trudged along in green wellies and Barbours, chatting happily to people they hadn't seen for years - and that included us - kicking snow off their boots and peering expectantly round this retail establishment that for most of them was as familiar as Tutenkhamen's tomb. People who as far as the shop was concerned could have been on lifelong hunger strikes were suddenly found to have gargantuan appetites. Butter ran out, bread ran out, eggs, bacon, cheese, coffee... We discovered items we didn't know we stocked and even *they* ran out.

The problem with such a surge of trade is that it can interfere with the requirements of regular customers. As the sugar supply was on the point of dwindling to zero, I rescued the last bag and put it behind my back. A woman saw me do this and asked for a bag of sugar.

"There's none left" was my untruthful but not unreasonable reply.

"Yes there is. You've got a bag behind your back."

"That's for Mrs. X."

She looked distinctly put out. "So it's not first come first served in this shop?"

I shrugged. "Sorry. I have to look after my regulars."

I should have said, "Yes it *is* first come first served. But MrsX has come before you in this shop about fifty thousand times. She uses us and supports us in fair weather and foul and I'll be buggered if I'm giving you *her* sugar on the one occasion you can't make it to Tesco's. It seems quite reasonable that I'll save our last bag of sugar for a customer who spends thirty odd pounds every week rather than one who spends the odd fiver once in a blue moon – or, more appositely, a white earth."

But I didn't say any of this. I just smiled sweetly, nursed my wicked thoughts and wished her a nice day. "See you next snowfall," I couldn't help adding as she left.

CHAPTER TWO

GOING.... GOING

I was amused to hear recently that BBC's Book of the Week was concerned with shopping instincts and had a title something like *Why People Buy* (that must have exercised someone's imagination.) We were pre-occupied with precisely the opposite: why people *don't* buy.

The threat to village shops can be summed up in three words - apathy, apathy, and....apathy. Secondary reasons can be suggested but in the final analysis looking outside the local community for reasons village shops fail is a red herring, an attempt to shift the blame. If the local community is serious about the shop's survival, the shop will survive.

But usually the local community isn't serious enough to make the necessary adjustments to its shopping habits and most village shops depend on an alarmingly small number of customers. The retired vicar and his wife used to spend £40 to £50 a week in the shop. Their successors spent nothing. A couple who used to spend all their weekly benefit in the shop moved to a nearby town and ninety pounds a week went into someone else's till. This is a fact of life for the village shopkeeper; customers leave, you hope others will emerge to replace them. And although we were rarely disappointed, our market base was always worryingly small consisting of Poulton and the surrounding villages with only around twenty five per cent of Poulton residents using the shop regularly and substantially.

An auctioneer used to live in the village. Three or four times a year he sent out mail shots which guaranteed us the sale of several thousand stamps, a not inconsiderable addition to our post office trade. Then he switched to a franking machine. Cheaper, quicker and more efficient, it was a change that made sense for him. We still took his mail for the postman to collect but now we made nothing from his business. His local post office had become a convenience rather than a business selling him a service.

This makes it sound as if our only consideration was profit which is not so. We were happy to take his letters but shops cannot survive as altruistic institutions and the pressure to deprive them of business is increasing all the time. Franking machines were a minor problem. More insidious is the ongoing campaign by Government to persuade recipients of benefits to have them paid directly into their bank accounts. When we first came to Poulton, our MP was Nicholas Ridley who, whatever his faults, was still a character, a national luminary. The MP who took over when Ridley retired was Geoffrey Clifton-Browne, a man who brings to mind an old quotation. *"He stood twice for Parliament but so diffidently that his candidature passed almost unnoticed."* One of his contributions to parliamentary debate was the erroneous statement that paying benefits directly into the recipient's bank account wouldn't affect subpostmasters' salaries. Luckily, the issue raised sufficient outcry for a campaign to be mounted urging pensioners and others to carry on collecting their benefits from the Post Office.

Other threats to the viability of the business, both post office and shop, came from utility companies offering discounts if payment was made by direct debit, the newspaper price war reducing the profits from newspaper sales, the high interest rates of the early nineties, and the indiscriminate application of the Uniform Business Rate. At the same time supermarkets bit deeply into profits and food hygiene regulations dramatically increased. Like a threatened species of wildlife, village shops dwindled to the point where extinction was a real possibility and many shuddered violently and gave up the ghost. The Government and local authorities lamented this and there was much weeping and wailing while at the same time politicians planned more cost-cutting schemes and local authorities approved applications for still more out-of-town superstores.

The arithmetic of village shop economics needs spelling out. Poulton is a village of around 150 families. If every family spent £10 a week in the shop the village would contribute a turnover of £1500 and on that figure, at a profit of around 18%, the gross income from the shop would be £270 a week. Added to the families who spent substantially more than £10 a week, the passing trade, the trade from neighbouring villages, and the post office salary, this kind of commitment would ensure that the shop was never under threat. But most families spent far less than £10 a week. Some didn't even spend £10 in the twelve years we were there. Many would buy the occasional pint of milk or something they'd forgotten to buy at the supermarket and as I've remarked elsewhere, this was like being members of a club without paying your fees, relying on others to keep it open so that the facilities were available when you needed them.

If a village shop closes, it isn't the proprietors who lose out. They are enterprising enough to move into other fields and the value of the freehold alone will usually preclude penury. It is the village that loses, the cohesion of the community that is under threat. No one would suggest that a village like Poulton could degenerate to the level of an inner city but the possibility of serious communal decline with the lowering of the quality of life - not to mention property prices - should at least give villagers who don't use their shops pause for thought.

The decline of village shops in the face of the supermarkets' advance is not just a simple case of customers wanting to save a few pounds. A recent snippet in the *Independent* pointed out that although pet food is cheaper in the local pet shop than at Sainsbury's, people still buy it at Sainsbury's because the pet shop doesn't sell groceries. So cost-cutting *and* convenience are the two considerations that lead shoppers to the supermarkets. Loyalty to a well-established and important village institution comes a poor third.

A classic case of this can be seen in a village in Pembrokeshire, close to where we have our holiday chalet. The village has two shops; a Spar mini-market where we buy our newspapers, food and cleaning items, and a bakery where we buy fresh bread. Recently, we were dismayed to see that the mini-market had opened an in-store bakery. Of course it is convenient for shoppers to buy their bread at the same time as they are buying other items but in the process the healthy profits of the mini-market are boosted at the expense of the shaky profits of the bakery. Poor Peter is being robbed to pay affluent Paul.

I would hope that the residents boycott the bread from the mini-market and carry on using their traditional bakery but I doubt whether in the end they will support it in sufficient numbers to keep it open. There is something inevitable about the advance of the multiples, their money not just talking but bellowing into the ear of any small retailer who might get in their way.

Perhaps small shopkeepers are like King Canute. Perhaps there is no way of preventing the tidal wave of "progress" sweeping over our little patch of sand. But we have to hope that enough people are both community-minded and can see the value of small retailers, otherwise rural and urban communities alike will continue to have the hearts torn out of them.

As I mentioned earlier, Poulton still has its village shop loyalists and their numbers remained fairly constant over the years. Some died and others moved on but they always seemed to be replaced. And the loyalists included some of the newcomers as well as the traditional residents. In fact some of the new arrivals chose to live in Poulton because it still had a shop while many of the people who have been here for years hardly used the shop at all. So the theory that village shops are under threat because of the changing rural population and the apathy of the incomers is not a theory we could support.

In any case, most of the villagers – old or new – relied on a small minority to keep the place open. As Churchill (almost) said: "never in the field of human retailing has so much been owed to so many by so few." I used to apply Oscar Wilde's definition of a cynic (someone who knows the price of everything and the value of nothing) to the free marketeers of the nineteen eighties but it applies equally to villagers who don't support their shops.

On paper at least, village shops are among the most valued of British institutions. Jeremy Fennel, Head of Rural Policy at ACRE (Action with Communities in Rural England) says that the greatest strength of village shops is "the familiar friendly face behind the counter, the personal attention and the time for a chat." Muriel Perks, a RDC advisor, agrees. "Village shopkeepers are at the heart of the community. They are someone to talk to, someone to notice if one of the locals hasn't been in for their bread and may be un-well. They provide a real neighbourhood watch, something that it would be very sad to lose."

But in spite of this raised profile, in spite of the goodwill of so many rural people and government departments, and in spite of the stated desire of all villages to retain their shops, the tide of closures continues. It is one of the paradoxes of rural life that virtually all villagers want to save their shops, but only a few will make the necessary adjustments to their shopping habits to do so.

To take an example of this, the Women's Institute recently submitted to the Government a report on the decline in rural amenities and the consequent downgrading of rural life. It included the recommendation that efforts were needed to save village shops. In the last few years we have been interviewed by several schoolchildren doing projects on village shops. (This in itself shows how the profile of village shops has been raised). The last time I was interviewed, the final question was "Do you think the Government should provide financial help to village shops?" My initial reaction was "Yes" but then I thought about it. No government can help a

USE IT OR LOSE IT....

non-viable institution indefinitely. The only people who can ensure the shop survives are *members of the local community*. They are its market and its survival is entirely in their hands. If the village supports it and is prepared to pay a little more for some provisions, the shop will survive. Otherwise, sooner or later it will go the way of others irrespective of whether or not the Government provides subsidies. So if your village shop is a lame duck, *only you and your neighbours can get it airborne again*. Incidentally, we found the concern of the Women's Institutes somewhat ironic in that members of the Poulton W.I. generally used the shop very little. Many people take up the slogan of "Save Our Shop" without realising that it has implications for their own behaviour.

CHAPTER THREE

RAISING THE PROFILE

Poulton Village Shop (Mr & Mrs SB Russell)
County Winner - Gloucestershire
IN THE 1996

COMPETITION

Sometime in the late 1960's, I heard that Cliff Richard had won the Eurovision Song Contest with *Congratulations*. "Good grief," I thought, "what must the other entries have been like?" Our less appreciative customers probably felt the same in 1996 when we were adjudged Gloucestershire's "Village Shop of the Year" in the competition organised by *Woman and Home* and Calorgas. We particularly hoped that the customer who had classed us as "Not at all satisfactory" in all aspects of the Post Office survey was aware of it.

Joking apart, the award was the pinnacle of our time in the shop and showed that our efforts to provide a high level of service hadn't gone unnoticed. We had been runners-up in 1994 and had now gone one better. We received a cheque for £50 and took Joyce out for a meal in recognition of her contribution. What was even more satisfying was to have won it on the strength of our customers' commendations. They couldn't have been commending us for opening hours, the tidiness of the establishment or the smartness of the staff so they must have placed a high value on the atmosphere in the shop and the "pastoral" dimension we tried to provide.

But if the organisers of the competition hoped that a successful shop would become a source of local pride which would result in increased support, in Poulton they would have been disappointed.

We received plaudits from our regulars - many of whose testimonials had been responsible for the award in the first place - and made the front page of the local paper, but for the bulk of the village, the shop remained as anonymous as ever and the award a matter of complete indifference.

This indifference apparently extended to the Parish Council. When an industry wins an export order, it is customary for the Government to send a letter of congratulations. We thought that, when we were declared "Gloucestershire's Village Shop of the Year", something similar might have been appropriate from the Parish Council. But then protocol might have demanded a letter of commiseration when we were robbed at gunpoint, a word of thanks when we retired after spending twelve years running an important village institution. In fact our retirement from Poulton Post Office was the only instance in many years of service in different parts of the world that we had left a job without even a letter to commemorate it.

But this is a small grouse and probably reveals that even at a local level, bureaucracy is incompatible with good public relations. We knew that the award was an achievement for the shop management *and* the village and it gave us and our supporters a great deal of satisfaction.

On a general level, the competition and a series of articles in *Woman and Home* raised the profile of village shops and again highlighted their importance. This was the culmination of several years of increasing village shop awareness. Successive governments opined their demise, the Rural Development Commission publicised their plight, and the Radio Four's *Today Programme* conducted an in-depth survey. Rural communities everywhere lamented the closures; letters were written, pressure groups organised and various ingenious schemes devised. Yet still the closures continued.

Some of the statistics are interesting. One survey estimated that 3,500 shops in England alone were under threat of closure and about half of all English village shops were up for sale. Of shopkeepers interviewed by the Sussex Rural Community Council, 40% expected to close within two years and in Kent and Surrey, the percentage was higher still.

In the early nineties, the Rural Development Commission started a number of initiatives to assist village shops. It expanded its retail advisory service, which sends consultants out to visit shopkeepers and gives advice on financing, merchandise and marketing. It organised seminars and was responsible for several publications including an open-learning package called *A Guide to Village Shopkeeping*, the pamphlet *Village Shops in Rural England* and a history of the village shop called simply *The Village Shop*. Finance was also made available and we received a grant for half the costs of re-vamping the shop - buying new vegetable and card racks and installing an upright fridge.

In addition, the Government authorised discretionary business rate relief for village shops and gave local authorities extra funds to achieve this. This was one of the few examples of the Government putting its money where its mouth was. The Uniform Business Rate was as ill thought out in its way as the poll-tax. All businesses throughout the country are charged not on their profits but on the square footage of their business property. A shop has a square footage quite out of proportion to its profits. We could have run an import-export agency turning over millions from one small room and paid a fraction of the rates we paid as a village shop.

The business rate was unfair on small shops for another reason. Small shops are not companies. The owners don't declare a divi-dend after paying all their expenses - including staff salaries - out of their profits. Their profits *are* their salaries and as, like the rest of the population, we paid the Council Tax this effectively meant we were paying *two* local government taxes out of our salaries. I argued this case to the Cotswold District Council and they used their discretionary powers to reduce our bill by fifty percent. In 1997, the incoming government went one better and authorised a hundred per cent relief. Eureka! Successive governments acting in the interests of village shops.

The Shop of the Year award was our most successful attempt to raise the shop's profile. Other ideas through the years had gener-ally come to nothing. At one point we considered changing the name of the shop. It occurred to us that for a post office stores situated in Poulton, the name *Poulton Post Office Stores* wasn't particularly imaginative or inspiring. One possible alternative was *The Eleventh Commandment* which would read something like "Thou shalt love and support thy shop with all thy heart and with all thy purse..." but the point was not so much what it meant as that it would get people talking. (Jeffrey Archer has since called one of his novels *The Eleventh Commandment* so perhaps it wasn't such a good idea). Another idea was to advertise local businesses over a tannoy system with me as a sort of Cotswold Jimmy Young or Henry Kelly playing customers' requests. We also thought of raffling a twenty-pound box of groceries each month with only customers who had spent above a certain amount eligible for the draw. The most satisfying idea was what we would do if we won the lottery. (Our chances are marginally less than other people's as we rarely buy a ticket). Everyone in the village would receive a letter saying a cheque was attached representing their level of support for the shop. Most cheques would be for £0.00. You see what nasty minds village shopkeepers have - even ones as nice as us!

From time to time we drew attention to the problems of village shops with articles and letters in the local press. In 1992, *The Wilts and Glos Standard* published a piece headed

USE YOUR SHOP OR LOSE IT

It made the usual points about the shop being the heart of the community, a place where people meet, gossip, exchange views and so on and ended

Before he took over at Poulton, another shopkeeper told Mr. Russell that the shop belonged to the village. "As long as the village shows that it wants a shop and gives you a reasonable living from it, you have a duty to keep it open. If not, you may have no option but to close it"

As a follow up to this article, I had a letter published in *Rural Voice* suggesting that residents of villages that still had a shop should ask themselves the following questions.

1. Do I personally feel that the village needs a shop and would be poorer without it?
2. Am I prepared to commit a substantial amount of weekly custom - to both shop and post office - to ensure it stays open?

The Rural Voice is circulated to all Parish Councils and we hoped - vainly as it turned out - that the Poulton Parish Council would take up cudgels on our behalf.

On the few occasions that business dipped to a level that caused concern, we appealed to the villagers for more support. The following was one such appeal.

£5 a week to save your village shop.

That's all it will take to ensure that Poulton village stores stays open FOREVER! £5 of custom each week from every adult in the village. Or £10 per family.
Isn't it worth spending this amount to ensure that the shop survives as a centre of village life and for the old and dependent people who really need us?

We listed our products and services, and mentioned the debt that Poulton owed to a handful of people whose efforts ensured that the village still had the convenience of the shop.

A few weeks later, after a lukewarm response, we sent out a follow up in which the final paragraph was the telling one:

Relying on a few customers to keep the shop open so that everyone can enjoy the benefits is a bit like using the facilities of a club without paying your fees. Please don't rely on others to keep the "club" open. Our assessment of the level of trade needed to keep the shop viable is premised on ALL Poulton residents using it. This doesn't just mean other people. IT ALSO MEANS YOU!

Using the facilities of a club without paying your fees is, I think, a fair comparison and I make no apologies for using it again. We even thought of revamping the old World War I poster with the face of Kitchener screaming "YOUR SHOP NEEDS YOU!"

Another of our initiatives was to test the belief that supermarket products were always cheaper than those bought locally. Feeling like a cross between industrial saboteurs and visitors to Disneyland, Lizzie and one of our village shop loyalists paid a visit to the local Tesco Superstore. All right if you like Disneyland, I suppose. They both hated it. But the purpose was less to pass judgement on the place than to compare prices. After a couple of hours and in spite of the attentions of some kind of store detective, they had what they wanted - a list of prices for items (carefully selected) that were also sold in our shop. The shopping basket cost £40.95 in Tesco, £41.47 in Poulton Post Office stores and we produced a circular showing the price comparison. The myth that supermarkets were always much cheaper had been shattered. If you are careful, shopping locally need not cost a lot more and for some products you may actually pay less.

The Tesco comparison was one of our more successful attempts at publicity. People could see that we were prepared to put in some work to attract customers and trade picked up substantially. We followed up the price comparison with other handouts. I wrote a cautionary tale about two sisters one of whom supported her village shop and one who thought she could leave it for a while - "Lord make me chaste but not yet" sort of thing. The day came when, snowbound and arthritic, she had no option but to limp along to her local shop. Shock horror! The shop had closed the week before. The doggerel ends with the cry:

> *I'd turn the clock back if I could*
> *But shops once closed are closed for good.*

And unlike other cautionary tales (the girl who cried, "Fire!" the boy who was eaten by a lion) this one rings only too true for many villages. Cries of anguish can be heard as another shop disappears into history. Ah, but did you support it when it was open? Well, we used to buy milk (when we'd run out), bread (when we'd forgotten to get some at the supermarket) and we always posted our letters there. Oh, and dad often popped in for his *Sun*.

Yes, I know all that, but did you support it?

And the answer has to be: "No. It supported you."

Cautionary tales are not always fictitious and we didn't have to look far for actual examples. In the mid-nineties, the shops at Ampney Crucis and Down Ampney - two villages a few miles from Poulton - both closed and the villages felt bereft. Ampney Crucis was particularly traumatised as its pub closed at the same time. Of course we benefited - particularly on the post office side - and the general feeling was that we must have been pleased. On one level we were but it was the level which finds solace when on the death of a relative, you inherit a bit of money. It's some small compensation for the loss. And we did feel a loss, a sense of be-reavement, when two members of our "post office family" were no longer there.

Some Poulton residents received news of the closures with foreboding but most still believed that we were somehow immune from the pressures which had caused so many of our colleagues literally to "shut up shop". "You'll never close," one of the never-buy-anything villagers said when I told him to heed the cautionary tales of the two local villages. "If it had been left to you we'd have closed years ago," I said but he left unconvinced. Or perhaps uninterested.

Down Ampney, like a few other villages, attempted to revive its shop on a community basis. Community shops range from stalls set up once a week in the village hall, to permanent shops financed and staffed by volunteers. Such attempts meet with mixed success. Many residents of Down Ampney still came to us but we were three miles away and for people without their own transport we might as well have been in Timbuktu. Such people need shops within walking distance. Community shops are a partial solution but they are nothing like as stable as permanent shops profession-ally run. Apart from Poulton, only three village shops now exist in the area, two thriving, one seriously threatened if the regular bleating of its owner is anything to go by.

Anyway, our advice to all rural communities is support your shop while you still have one. Apart from anything else, your shopkeepers might well win the lottery one day, and you wouldn't want to be one of the people receiving a cheque for £0.00.

Would you?

Occasional articles in the national press do village shopkeepers few favours. One such article appeared in *The Independent* in 1997. It was called "Serious Shopping" and written by someone called Philip Delves Broughton. (Is that a name or a sentence?). His opening was an instant alienator:

> *Nostalgia aside, there is little reason why anyone would want to shop in village shops. Unless of course they live on a diet of overpriced corned beef, sponge fingers and stale sugar puffs. Village shops are poorly stocked, overpriced and no contest for the air-conditioned, wide-aisled pleasure of out-of-town supermarkets.*

Then, having made derogatory remarks about the *pathetic attempts* of some village shops to turn themselves into feeble imitations of the urban delicatessen, selling *limp lemon grass or curling Parma ham with the owners like awkward farmhands at the Squire's table*, he goes on to explain that at least one village shop is bucking the trend calling it *"a rustic delicatessen ... steeped in sponge-fingered tradition. This may be the future for the village shop... the way to cock their villagey snook at the corporate retailing monsters hungry for their business."*

Far from very few village shops being on the right path, many have realised for years that they can survive only by providing a different kind of service from the "corporate retailing monsters". Mr Delves Broughton makes a mistake that serious analysts shouldn't make. He presents an "either..or" rather than a "both..and" situation. In addition he fails to acknowledge that the kind of shop that can survive is the post office store because it has a guaranteed, if modest, salary. His "Nostalgia aside..." opening is particularly galling. People who suddenly want a loaf of bread don't go to the village shop out of a longing for the past, neither do old people without their own transport, or villagers who want a paper delivered, or inefficient shoppers who've left a couple of items off their supermarket list and can't be bothered to make another trip to Tesco's, tempting though the thought of those "wide, air-conditioned aisles" might be.

Perhaps we should have sent Delves Broughton our "Poulton Post Office Recipes" compiled by one of our loyalists who is also a gourmet cook, and who, for dinner parties, bought many of her ingredients from the village shop. And I don't think she used corned beef, sponge fingers or sugar puffs (either the stale or fresh varieties) very often. Or limp lemon grass or curling Parma ham either, come to that.

I referred earlier to our "Tesco Comparison". Perhaps this might be the place to make a few other observations about those places that offer this wide-aisled splendour. Yes, supermarkets have caused a serious decline in local trade. Yes, there is something unethical about their loss leaders, their undercutting of prices, their ruthless and incessant attempts to corner the market in everything from petrol to pharmaceuticals, newspapers to bread. And yes, the number of local businesses of all types that have been destroyed by their advance makes horrific reading. If I steal money from our baker, I shall probably be sent to prison. If I open a supermarket and lure customers by offering bread at less than the profitable selling price thereby depriving the baker of a large chunk of money *every* day until he is forced into closure, I shall be termed a shrewd businessman. Soon there will be no choice and the vulnerable and dependent, as well as the people who hate supermarket shopping, will be marooned in the world of wide-aisled splendour.

But, unpalatable though it may be for small shopkeepers, supermarkets are a fact of life. They may be superseded as the blood circulates in different patterns through the retail system but for the present village shops have to live with them or die. And living with them needn't be so bad as long as we are adaptable. It is their voracious appetites that make them so undesirable. Nobody seems to approve of them very much but everyone shelves this disapproval when it comes to saving a few pence and having the convenience of doing all their shopping in one place. And in fairness, they offer a variety and a freshness that is often lacking in village shops.

So living with them means competing on different terms. Although for many items (by no means all) supermarkets are cheaper, shopping there is often more expensive because of the temptation to buy things that weren't planned and aren't needed. Every day in our shop, mothers had to be firm with children who demanded the sweets that rotted their teeth or the chocolate that converted a becoming plumpness into a weight problem. In supermarkets there are more temptations, the time in the store is longer, there isn't a friendly shopkeeper to take the mother's side or divert the children while she is shopping. Her trolley is likely to be loaded with impulse buys that will add pounds to her bill and even more to her family's weight. So while individual items may be cheaper, supermarket shopping is not necessarily more cost-effective. In addition, people who live in villages can't walk to the supermarket and a trip of ten miles will add around £4 in motoring expenses to the cost of the goods even assuming that parking is free and your time worth nothing

So comparing village shops with supermarkets is not comparing like with like. Both should have their part to play in the great retail ecosystem but while both have retailing features, they are totally distinct species. In *Notes from a Small Island*, Bill Bryson says the best thing about the seaside resort of Morecambe was that it wasn't Blackpool. In the same way, the best thing about village shops is that they are not supermarkets. They should be offering something different and glorying in this fact. As Bryson said, it was a mistake when Morecambe tried to become another Blackpool. In fact, when Morecambe tried to make itself into another Blackpool, it wasn't being Wise (ugh!)

Village shops may well become fashionable again when retail trends change. We can see the start of a new trend with online shopping and perhaps within a few years those impregnable superstores will have been replaced - certainly as geographical entities - and the real estate they represent will be put to other uses. Then there will be no popping back to Tesco's for something you've forgotten. Most grocery orders will be delivered and local shops will cater for the amnesiacs and the computer illiterates. And like the Soviet Union which we also assumed was impregnable, those giants of Twentieth Century retailing will be consigned to history.

To end this chapter on a lighter note, Tom Boyd, an enterprising American with a flair for the theatrical, produced two shows in the village hall in 1995 and 1996 and the village shop featured in both. In the first, a scenario was created - not entirely imaginary - in which there was animosity between the postmaster and the proprietor of the local pub parodying the feud between the Farmer and the Cowman in *Oklahoma*. I quote just one verse:

> TOM: *I'd like to say a word for the postman*
> *To have a village shop is such a boon.*
>
> ME: *When you're out of eggs and ham*
> *Or you're desperate for some jam*
>
> BARMAN: *That's the day the shop is closed all*
> *afternoon!*

The last line, delivered though it was by the least competent member of the cast, received the loudest cheer in the show. I didn't realise so many residents had a craving for ham and eggs on Thursday afternoons. Perhaps the village was happier when Rob opened every afternoon as well as lunchtime though strangely, his sales of ham, eggs and jam hardly increased at all.

The second show saw Lizzie and me "starring" together, and gave me the chance to be a lyricist. I revamped the old favourite "Daisy Daisy" and called it "A Post Office made for Two." Among the lines were "We'll go to the cash and carry/The day before we marry", "You'll be queen behind the screen/Of a post office made for two," as well as the immortal "We'll do our best not to hate those/Who shop at Tesco and Waitrose," (well *I* think it's immortal.)

Not exactly the stuff to make the great lyricists tremble in their shoes perhaps (though a few might be turning in their graves). But not bad for someone who, when all's said and done, was only the local postmaster.

CHAPTER FOUR.

THE SOCIAL DIMENSION

Running a village shop involves a raft of responsibilities that extend beyond retailing into a whole range of things that can best be classified as social duties. Village shopkeepers are one of the last bastions of unpaid service. I naturally exclude the voluntary sector from this. The voluntary sector is peopled by saints and angels and village shopkeepers are neither saints nor angels.They are just people who because of their position in the community are among the first to hear of difficulties and take it upon themselves to help. Over time, this pastoral element – as one of our customers described it – is added seamlessly to their range of duties.

While we ran the shop, a great many personal tragedies came to our notice, most of them too private and distressing to be publicised. But we can describe one case if only because it had a happy outcome.

When we first came to Poulton, we gradually became aware of a lean, military-looking man wearing a camel-hair overcoat and an RAF tie, with a clipped moustache and a red nose. We'll call him Percy and he shared a house with his sister, went to the pub at lunchtimes, came to the shop every day for cigarettes and gin, collected his pension on Thursdays, and took the *Express*. At the time the *Express* seemed to be read by people who, to quote John Osborne, were "still dreaming of the their days among the Indian princes and unable to believe they'd left their horsewhips at home." Percy was always immaculately dressed and his concern with his appearance and personal hygiene reminded me of the Kipling line: "Always keep your rifle and yourself just so".

So we formed an impression of Percy as a man of old-fashioned values - not all of them by any means to be scorned, of independent means, certain to have a private pension and private health insurance, who liked his drink and who, in this area at least, didn't practise moderation.

Almost all our assumptions were wrong.

One day I gave him a lift into town and had my first intimation that all was not well. I knew that his sister was becoming increasingly infirm and would soon be moving into a home but until then I didn't know how this would affect her brother. I'd never spoken to him on personal matters but during that car journey, I discovered that he had no right of tenure. His sister had the right to live in the house as long as she wished but he was there only at her discretion.   As the time approached for her departure, Percy, a man in his mid-eighties, faced the prospect of being turned out on to the street.

He told me a lot during that trip into town and, with the ice broken, told me a great deal more. I learned that he had only his state pension to live on, that he had no family apart from his sister, a daughter in Canada and a brother somewhere on the South coast. He was going into town to discuss moving into a home himself, a prospect he viewed with unalloyed dread.The thought of leaving all his life support systems in Poulton was bad enough, but the idea of moving into a home was even worse.His pension would be taken to help pay the fees and he would be given £15 a week "pocket money". "Like a little boy" he said. "It'll hardly keep me in cigarettes." But the worst thing was the thought of "being stuck with all those old people. I'll be dead within six months."

Fate moves in strange ways. The same day I noticed that the flat opposite the post office was being prepared for letting and, after speaking to the landlord, I persuaded him to reserve it as a possible home for Percy. Percy was worried that he had no money for rent and no furniture. I was sure these obstacles could be overcome and he agreed to the move in principle. His doubts were probably the result of being unable to believe that someone was actually trying to help him. I then explained the position to the local housing officer and within a week Percy received notification that he was entitled to housing benefit and income support. He was also given financial help by Poulton's Allotment Trust (a trust specifically established for the relief of hardship in the village) and the Royal Airforce Benvolent Fund. After the lease had been signed, Barbara McIntyre and Lizzie purchased the necessary household items while I collected items of furniture from the volunteer bureau. On moving day, we helped Percy with his conveniently small hoard of personal belongings - two suitcases and a couple of paper bags were all he had to show for eighty six years on God's earth - and he became independent for the first time in many years.

The change in him was startling. He developed a self-confidence which we had never seen before and he started to smile. For ourselves, we felt satisfied that we had helped a proud old man recover his dignity and re-establish himself in the village that had become his home.

But moments of bliss tend to be shortlived. Unfortunately, the landlord didn't have the same concern for his welfare as the rest of the village. The heating failed and a cold, damp flat was no fit place for anyone let alone for a man now close to his ninetieth birthday. The last straw came when he received an eviction order, legally permissible but morally reprehensible particularly as it was due to take effect during November. After pressure from a few benevolent residents, the order was rescinded but it brought home to us that we couldn't rely on a private landlord to guarantee Percy's welfare. We now did what we should have done originally and registered him with the local housing association. Because of his age, he was given priority and a couple of months later he was allocated a centrally-heated bungalow in a quiet cul-de-sac in the village where he could stay as long as he chose.

Since 1994, Percy has been very much under our wing although we don't see as much of him since we left the shop. He occasionally asks for our help in dealing with the plethora of Council bureaucracy that pours through his letter box. At ninety one he neither has the inclination nor the mental capacity to understand the tortuous meanderings of the bureaucratic mind. Now if he was forty one....he still wouldn't understand it. I help him by throwing all the forms in the bin. Percy is also helped by one of his neighbours, a delightful man, made even more delightful by the fact that he shares our attitudes, uses the shop on a daily basis, and laughs at my jokes (particularly because he laughs at my jokes). He lives with and cares for his invalid mother and no favour is too much for him.

So Percy is now settled. I talk to him about various issues and he has a fund of knowledge on many interesting subjects. Most of his attitudes are as liberal as those of any other ninety-one-year old *Express* reader with an RAF background but when people need help, you give it without inquiring into their attitudes and prejudices.

Percy has many attributes but the ability to cope with modern technology isn't one of them. Trying to make him understand how to operate his TV with the remote control unit makes me appreciate my children's frustration at my inability to come to terms with the video. To Percy, pre-tuning the TV is an act of magic which only a technocratic wizard (i.e. me) could perform and which is certainly beyond ordinary mortals (i.e. him). He gives me an illusion of super-competence in a myriad different ways, such as his legendary inability to cope with voicemail. The following is a fair representation of what I have occasionally found on my answer phone:

Operator:	*You were called today at 5.54 pm. Would you like to play that message ??*
Me:	*Yes.*
Percy:	*Stuart!!!*

There follows an extended fit of spluttering and coughing during which every vestige of phlegm is removed from its anchorage deep in his throat and he manages to utter not a single word.

Operator: *Would you like to save that message?*

But we gained a lot of satisfaction from helping Percy settle into a life of comparative independence and have related it in detail because we think it provides another compelling example of why village shops are worth saving. If the shop hadn't been there, his predicament might never have come to anyone's notice.

Another instance of the shop running errands of mercy concerned a nice old woman, Miss Warwick, who lived in a remote hamlet a few miles from the village. Two or three times a week she would trundle to the shop in her rusty old car to buy groceries and food for her dog. As the years passed she became increasingly arthritic until she was unable to make the journey. She would give us her order by phone and we would deliver it.

Her house had no heating apart from an open fire and an electric heater and in the winter I used to take bags of coal with her groceries. Once when she phoned to say she was out of coal, snow had made the lanes off the main roads almost impassable for ordinary vehicles. I explained the situation to a well-heeled man with a four-wheel drive. He lived en route to Miss Warwick's house and I asked if he would deliver the coal, as I might find it difficult in my car. He refused and confirmed what I had long suspected; that there is an institutionalised lack of Christian values among some of the middle and upper middle classes of British society.

So it was left to me to set off into a white wilderness and try and avoid the ice and drifts. After a hazardous journey, I reached the house and found Miss Warwick huddled in front of the smallest fire imaginable, an eighty-year-old woman in need of the help that one allegedly Christian man had refused to provide. When I left she had a roaring fire and I had the satisfaction of having made a fellow human being's life more tolerable. It was a good feeling and one that I and the rest of the world should experience more often.

A little while after this, a middle-aged couple appeared in Miss Warwick's life, collecting her pension and doing her bits of shopping. The woman, soft-spoken and full of concern, referred to Miss Warwick as "Auntie". They had moved in with her ostensibly to make her final years more comfortable.

A year or so later we were informed that Auntie had died. We never heard from the couple again and knew nothing about them except that they lived with Miss Warwick. And stayed on in the house after she died.

On one occasion, I was quite overcome by the degree of authority a village postmaster exercises. One of our customers had been taken into hospital and her sister informed us that the doctors had given her only a few days to live. I told her to tell her sister to pull herself together. She lived for another four years! For the first time in my life I felt my achievements were at last commensurate with my abilities!

Since retirement, we hear little of the problems affecting people in the community. Selling the shop meant giving up both the commercial and the pastoral elements of the position. We still sometimes run the shop when Rob and Sue want a break and these stand-in periods emphasise how out-of-touch we've become. During one of them, I saw the sister of the sick woman and told her that I was thinking of paying her sister a visit.

"You're a bit late," she replied. "She's been dead three months."

CHAPTER FIVE

MASTERS OF BUREAUCRACY

You can't teach an old dogma new tricks (Dorothy Parker).

Many years ago in Kenya, a friend and I had finished a round of golf and were having a drink in the clubhouse. We ordered two beers and the waiter asked us to write the order down. My friend refused saying "You can remember two beers." I should explain that the club had recently introduced a policy of writing orders down because there had been so many complaints about wrong orders. Putting *large* orders in writing was sensible. But two beers!
"The trouble with the world today" my friend said "is that instead of doing useful jobs, most of us are just filling in bits of paper."
Now why does this story lead me to the Post Office?

In a post office stores, the shop and the post office are two sides of the same coin. One couldn't survive without the other yet the two couldn't be more different. The shop belonged to us and perhaps in a different way, to the village; the post office was managed by us yet in no real way belonged to us. It belonged to a government department which due to the re-organisation of recent years had become increasingly faceless. When we became subpostmasters in 1986, we had friendly and supportive visiting officers who came from head office in Gloucester. Within a year we knew more than half a dozen of them. A few years later and the umbilical cord had been cut. Mother Gloucester was no more and visits became a rarity. The telephone helpline was always there for advice but the previous feeling of companionship and tolerance disappeared. We were grateful for the presence in the area of other post offices where we could go for advice and occasional help when our second class stamp supply had been denuded by a customer demanding two thousand at a days' notice. But eventually two of those disappeared.

The Post Office is making a determined effort to move from the nineteenth to the twenty first century in one leap, showing a belated awareness of changing lifestyles by offering services such as foreign currency and travel insurance and introducing swipe cards for utility payments. There are still some anachronisms, such as our main tool of trade, the date stamp, which is still inked manually, changed manually and is probably the most archaic piece of equipment in use anywhere outside the Sudan. If postmasters want a self-inking date stamp they have to find over a hundred pounds to buy one. But in spite of this, the Post Office is trying hard to modernise its image. It has even started to computerise the network though the programme, "Horizon", is predictably having problems. The name symbolises the fact that the Post Office has stopped contemplating its navel and is looking ahead. But even this symbol is flawed as farsighted organisations can see *beyond* the horizon. Still credit where credit's due. For an institution that has frequently failed to spot the end of its nose, "Horizon" is a quantum leap. Yet for all its efforts, the Post Office consistently fails in the two areas in which it has always failed: bureaucracy and jargon.

It has also acquired a more up-to-date problem in that it now equates accountancy with efficiency. This elevation of accounting into pole position commits a basic error when applied to the Post Office. Although many rural offices, judged by strict business accounting, are operating at a loss, there is an extensive service element, which is difficult to present in conventional profit and loss terms. How do you quantify the advantages a village gets from having a post office and shop - the two invariably go together? How do you quantify the benefits that society at large gains from having a series of communities - instead of a series of non-communities - which village post offices help to sustain? How do you quantify the social and financial benefits that result from shops and post offices taking on policing, counselling, and communication responsibilities? If we are to make a proper evaluation of a particular post office, we either have to introduce a dimension other than the financial one or find a way of costing these "non-profitable" benefits. Even imponderables such as helping old ladies across the road or being available for a chat to someone feeling depressed would have to be given a value. I question our ability to do this; there are surely some things that can't be evaluated in financial terms

In addition to the social function performed by each post office, the very size of the network gives it an economic value far above the sum total of business that each office conducts. A network of 18000 outlets is attractive to all kinds of enterprises. It is an extensive circulation system with capillaries energising the remotest areas of the country. A company looking for an agency is more likely to be attracted to a network that reaches into remote areas than one where all the non-profitable offices have been closed. I hope the Government has the potential of the network in mind when it talks of the need to give greater commercial freedom and opportunities. I hope it isn't just another exercise in "spinning"(horrible word) and that behind the scenes, the Post Office isn't being made "leaner and fitter" as a prelude to a sell-off.

This lack of confidence in government intentions was partly induced by some of the statements made by politicians. For example, Michael Heseltine, in his capacity of President of the Board of Trade, dismayed us by his comment that he wasn't considering the privatisation of Post Office Counters "because sub post offices are privatised already."

Perhaps this was simply an off-the-cuff remark in the Commons that hadn't been thought through, but it just wasn't true. Sub post offices are *not* privatised. It is true that many share premises with a business that *is* private but this is a different matter. In fact a comparison between the two co-habiting businesses is revealing.

Private businesses are run at the discretion of their owners within the law of the land. As far as the shop was concerned, we chose our own opening hours, decided what goods we sold, and completed the extraneous activities involved in running the business in our own time and at our own pace. If we decided through laziness or other commitments to leave our accounts for two or three weeks - or two or three months - that was up to us and we completed them on any paper and in any manner we chose. We could also take money from the business - as long as we recorded it as personal drawings.

Compare this to the post office. The position of subpostmaster is a civil service appointment. When a subpostmaster resigns, regulations demand that the position is advertised for a certain length of time and theoretically anyone can apply. In reality only one person *will* apply but the whole bureaucratic charade has to be gone through. Then after his appointment, a subpostmaster is told what business he is allowed to conduct, during what hours he will conduct it, what forms he will conduct it on, when and where he will make his application for cash or stock, on what day he will complete his weekly accounts, and what transactions are to be accounted for every day and those that are dealt with weekly. His salary is paid monthly like any other employee and Class 1 National Insurance is deducted.

Given the nature of the Post Office, most of these arrangements may well be necessary, but to call us private businesses is misleading. We are no more private businesses than a teacher in a school is a private business just because he has control over his classroom.

Successive governments have made it increasingly difficult for Post Office Counters Limited in that all profits go to the Treasury. If Post Office Counters was private, the Treasury would take its usual tax cut and the rest would be given as dividends or ploughed back into the business. Then innovations like the computerisation programme could be completed. For all these reasons, Mr. Heseltine's claim that Post Office Counters was already in the private sector was absurd.

One way in which the Post Office will never change is in the proliferation of bureaucracy. It has long been the acknowledged master of bureaucratic techniques and continues to extend the frontiers of bureaucracy beyond the wildest dreams of the most pedantic civil servant. In the ideology of the Post Office, the efficiency of the operation seems to be measured by the volume of paper used. A few years ago, Michael Heseltine (that man again) promised to cut through the red tape that clogged so many business operations. So by now you would perhaps have expected the Post Office, world leader in state of the art bureaucracy (i.e. never using one form when several will do) to have benefited from the new directives.

Not a bit of it.

New forms for new transactions proliferate, new forms for old transactions proliferate. One wall of our storeroom was covered with post office stationery, most of which we would never use but hadn't the confidence to throw away.

On several occasions I asked the Post Office not to treat us as if we were a small version of an urban office particularly with regard to the supply of DSS forms and leaflets. Literature explaining the different benefits is sent out irrespective of the size of post office or the area it serves. So while Poulton is full of people who regularly invest in Premium Bonds and National Savings Certificates, not too many villagers receive family credit or income support. Yet for years we received as many leaflets as an office in an area of high unemployment and ninety percent of them went straight into the recycling bag. Multiply this several times a year by the number of offices in the network and you begin to wonder how many forests are being sacrificed to this exercise in redundancy. In fairness, the Post Office did eventually rationalise the supply but this rationalisation should have taken place years before. Apart from environmental considerations, many offices don't have the time or the space to wade through new leaflets or display new advertising material - which is frequently only an update of old advertising material anyway. A recent audit revealed that only ten percent of offices were displaying all the correct posters and more than twenty percent were displaying no correct posters at all. Which rather negates the point of the posters, or perhaps proves that posters have little bearing on the capacity of an office to operate efficiently.

The same principle applied to the supply of stationery. In our "standard pack", delivered twice a year, there were forms we never used. Again a perfectly usable form would suddenly be declared obsolete and the hundreds we had left would be binned as a new number and design took its place. There are people working on these new designs who think they're doing an important job - and probably earning more than the average   subpostmaster for doing it.

Next we come to the question of jargon. Many years ago when I was a National Service sergeant, one of my colleagues was a blunt Lancastrian called Jim Gregory. Jim was the quartermaster sergeant and his language was a fascinating mixture of the barrackroom and the stores. Never one to ration his Anglo-Saxon, he would suddenly bawl out to a recruit with a light bulb in his hand "Oy, where the f... are you going with that lamps electric?" His jargon, never in any sense clear, scaled new heights during a kit check and he would bark at a bemused barrack room "Drawers cellular, 1947 issue, pairs three" which I had to interpret as three pairs of underpants.

No connection with the modern, dynamic Post Office? Consider the following examples (selected from many). One morning a large brown envelope arrived in the post containing a single sheet of paper with the words "Emergency Cascade" in big black letters. My first thought was that a river had burst its banks (there *had* been a lot of rain about) and that the public was being asked to contribute to a relief effort. Or perhaps it referred to food being dropped into somewhere like Southern Sudan. Reading on, I discovered that "Emergency Cascade" was actually a synonym for "Urgent Notice". In fact, "Urgent Notice" was written in minute letters underneath just in case there was the odd reader who might have needed a translation.

Another example occurred when my stepson, a young barrister, was working on a case of Girobank fraud and phoned to ask what a roundel was. This was a new one on us so I asked Rob who was equally puzzled. We eventually deduced that roundel must be another word for date stamp and so it proved. But an investigation was interrupted, an unnecessary phone call made and twenty minutes of a barrister's time wasted simply because Girobank didn't use the familiar and universal term "date stamp." Girobank is of course no longer officially part of the Post Office but one can't help thinking that some of the latter's ambience still lingers. Bureaucratic habits (i.e. never use a familiar word when an unfamiliar one will serve the same purpose) die hard.

"Emergency Cascade" for "Urgent Notice", "Roundel" for "Date stamp"? After that, "drawers, cellular, pairs three" is a segment of a sweet, circular food item. Or, to put it more prosaically, a piece of cake.

In one *Counters Bulletin* selected at random, I came across the following little mind twister relating to scratch cards:

> *If you activate packs of Payout 2001 after 3rd March 1999*
> *you must accept liability for any unsold activated stock at*
> *Camelot Game End.*

In the same Bulletin, there was an item relating to the "Driving Licence Application Form Destruction Certificates". All offices had to complete a Driving Licence Application Form Destruction certificate, *including the offices that didn't actually stock Driving Licence Application Forms*. The certificates then had to be sent to the "Driving Licence Application Forms Destruction Certificate Team". They actually had an official team certifying that offices, even those not stocking the item, had destroyed all obsolete stock, by which they meant the previous edition of the Driving Licence Application Forms, which could presumably have gone on forever. It makes the jettisoning of a yoghurt two days past its sell-by date almost sensible. The Post Office also supplies a "Jargon Buster" which begs the question that if jargon needs explaining and can be explained in simple terms, why is it used in the first place?

Another distinctive aspect of the Post Office is its fluency in bureauspeak. You can always tell a genuine Post Office person - within days of taking up employment they use bureauspeak like a native. Consider the facility with which they refer to every one of the plethora of forms by its number, the following being only too typical:

Phone rings. "Chesterfield here" "As in "Lord," I'm sometimes tempted to say but let it pass. Literary allusions are not their strong point. As in "P787/3(f)" would probably induce the response "Spot on."

"Is that 363 471 8?"

"Yes."

"Do you have your DNS 56 for week 16?"

"I don't know. Explain what it is and I'll tell you."

"I've told you what it is. It's your DNS 56."

"For Week 16?"

"Exactly."

"I'm still not sure."

"Never mind. You'll have transferred the figures to
  P885390126(16)

"If you say so."

"Either will do."

"What exactly do you want?"

"The figures from your DNS 56 for..."

"Could you translate into English?"

"We're not allowed. Anyone caught speaking English will
  have forty lashes with a fortified P884. It's dealt with in
  Counters Guide Number 16, Section 2 (a) amendment xii.).
  Read it if you don't believe me."

All right, so I exaggerate. There's nothing about forty lashes (it's two score flagellatory strikes).

Why can't they speak normally? If it was easier for communication to take place by making extensive use of numbers, it would be a defining characteristic of all languages. We don't call chairs Ch 24's and tables T68's because we've realised that's not the best way to communicate. Using numbers instead of words is stilted and artificial and there's absolutely no need for it. "Have you got your National Savings Bank summary form?" is just as easy to say as "Have you got your DNS56?" and infinitely easier to remember. Suffice it to say that Lizzie and I never mastered bureauspeak which meant that the Post Office always retained something of the aura of a foreign country. In fairness, it's not only the Post Office that uses bureauspeak. Worryingly it has spread into many other areas of life. The ultimate absurdity is seen in website addresses: double you double you double you is nine syllables; World Wide Web is three. Yet everyone uses the nine-syllable version.

Post Office Counters shared its headquarters in Gloucester with the Royal Mail at Royal Mail House (now there's an imaginative name). Seeing the building for the first time I was struck by the number of windows. Given that most windows represented offices, I concluded that the range of activities that went on in Royal Mail House must be awesome. (Remember this was before I knew anything about the Post Office and realised that eighty per cent of the people lurking behind those windows were doing nothing but filling in bits of paper. Many of them were probably occupied by teams similar to the Driving Licence Application Destruction Certificate Team mentioned earlier).

Another irritating habit of the Post Office was the presentation of new business as exciting opportunities for subpostmasters. Most new business was nothing of the kind. It simply meant extra work for very little reward. Scratch cards were a case in point. A rural post office receives, say, a hundred scratch cards, retailing at £1 each and giving the postmaster ten percent profit. If he sells ten a week, he makes £1.00 - or £52 a year. For this, he has to order stock, count it, stamp each card, keep the cards safe, pay out and account for small winners (in our experience there were *only* small winners), enter them on his stock sheet each week and order more when they run out. Yet scratch cards are presented as a business opportunity. The same applies to other new business such as Travel Insurance and Foreign Exchange. Offering these items is a great feather in POCL's cap. Clients are impressed with the 18,000 outlets and POCL gets a correspondingly better deal. But it is not a better deal for the rural postmaster. For each new "business opportunity", he has to attend seminars, train his staff, learn the accounting and documentation procedures, and all for perhaps a dozen transactions a year. These new transactions are opportunities all right but not for the rural subpostmaster. They are opportunities for POCL, crown offices and the larger suburban offices. They are a similar scam to network marketing where on the basis of maximum effort for minimal rewards, a lot of people make a lot of money for a few.

I recently saw a directive from the Post Office relating to personal appearance and dress - no hair colours that don't approximate to natural shades, no shorts, and only one piece of facial jewellery. Whether this offends against the law on personal freedoms is debatable. What is beyond dispute is that the person who laid down these rules had never seen a meeting of subpostmasters. It's a feat beyond even my imagination to visualise your average subpostmaster with green hair, a coxcomb and a couple of rings through his nose. He typically wears bifocals, conservative ties, dark trousers and possibly a V-neck pullover. His greying hair is neatly parted and he is clean-shaven. In other words the rules are redundant, slightly offensive and possibly illegal which just about sums up the Post Office's dealings with its staff.

I wonder what they have to say about dressing gowns. Not that I ever appeared on duty in my dressing gown but I usually wore it to put up the paper rounds and on some Saturdays even delivered a couple of papers in it. But one Sunday morning, when Marlene was running the shop, I got caught out. I needed an accounts book from the upstairs store at the back of the shop. Peeking into the shop and seeing no customers, I dashed through and up the ladder but before I could get back, a customer came in for his paper. Normally, he would have been dealt with in a few seconds but he decided to query his bill and by the time he had finished, the shop was full and I was marooned in the back for nearly half an hour.

The organisation that supposedly looks after postmasters in their dealings with the Post Office is the National Federation of Subpostmasters. I've related elsewhere how longstanding grievances of subpostmasters such as the holiday substitution allowance haven't been addressed but a measure introduced in the last few years underlines the inadequacy of the Federation in getting a fair deal for subpostmasters and allowing them to be subjected to terms of employment that no other professional person would tolerate. This is the so-called "take-over" fee.

When an office changes hands, if the salary is above a certain level - an arbitrary cut off point, which I believe, is currently £12,000 - the incoming postmaster takes a twenty five per cent non-refundable cut in his first year's salary. The Post Office's rationalisation for this monstrous levy is that it caters for time wasters - postmasters who leave after a year or so - and ensures the Post Office covers the cost of their training period. In theory this is unobjectionable. But in practice it doesn't just penalise time wasters. It penalises *all* subpostmasters in offices earning above £12000 a year, and none in offices earning below £12000 a year. Why not repay the money once an appointee has proved his reliability by completing two years service - 20% repaid in the third year, 30% in the fourth and 50% in the fifth?

Can you imagine any other job where a successful applicant would forfeit forever 25% of the first year's salary agreed for that post? The situation becomes even more absurd in that a salary of

£11,999 would be paid in full whereas a salary of £12,000 would be reduced to £9000. Unbelievable? Not in the looking-glass world of POCL.

After the first few months, we rarely attended Federation meetings which must have been a big disappointment to our predecessor who was the chairman of the local branch and I think hoped I would continue the Poulton dynasty. Apart from recognising the futility of many of the meetings and the weakness of the Federation to effect change, we also recognised something else at those early meetings: tedium. Boredom hung like a smoke haze over the whole gathering. We listened to a few uninspired speakers giving vent to a plethora of grievances some of which were too puny to be taken seriously, heard a Post Office representative respond, retired to uninspiring sandwiches and worse coffee and went home feeling the mental numbness that follows an evening of unrelieved boredom. My memory of those meetings was of a group of middle-aged men and women whose preoccupations could have been cloned. These were people who lived, breathed and dreamed the Post Office. We couldn't see the point of giving up our time to listen to someone arguing the case for an extra point for cashing a pension docket. Even if the Post Office was convinced by such claims, the net difference in income would have been about £20 a year - which would no doubt be clawed back in other ways. Again, I suppose the difference between us and many subpostmasters was that they were professionals in every sense of the word. And while we did the job to the best of our ability, we never saw it as a career, much less a "calling."

I'm sure this attitude was clear in our dealings with the auditors. The auditors were a species of Post Office personnel whose only purpose in life seemed to be to persecute, or more specifically to persecute me. They would arrive unannounced just before opening time, hawkeyed creatures who flashed their identity cards and demanded access to the intimacies and vagaries of the post office accounts. Then they would sniff around for several hours with the air of people who know there's something there if only they're sharp enough to find it while I skulk like a guilty schoolboy wondering why I can no longer see over the tops of the island units in the shop (it's because I've moved into furtive mode and shrunk to half my normal size). At the end, they have a short talk with me and having found little amiss, pass a reluctant verdict of not proven. Then like lions that have somehow missed out on an easy kill, they slope off to pursue other prey.

All auditors were like this except one.

One day a small, meek man was fluttering outside when we opened and when he said he was an auditor I couldn't believe my ears. Or my luck. No need for furtive mode here. I drew myself up to my full height and handed over the records. A few hours later he handed them back having discovered the accounts fifty pounds short and six motor vehicle licences not accounted for. And *he* apologised to *me*! I felt a great surge of brotherly love for this man and wondered how he could possibly have become an auditor. He seemed as out of place as a pacifist in a gang of street fighters.

In the post office, as in the shop, the customers were the redeeming feature and although post office work generally precluded the cavalier approach we sometimes used in the shop, we were always looking for ways of lifting the bureaucratic haze. April Fool's Day was one excuse to indulge ourselves and some of this indulgence centred round customers buying motor vehicle licences, many of whom had only the vaguest notion of what documents they needed. So they were fair game on 1st April.

One woman was speechless when I said her insurance certificate was out-of-date. She looked hard at it and then back at me.

"It isn't."

"It is," I said, taking the certificate from her. "Look"

"It says it's valid until 15th August, l995."

"It's out-of-date."

"It isn't."

"It is."

She shook her head. "One of us is crazy, and I don't think it's me."

I sighed. "What's today's date?"

"1st April . So if it expires in August it must still be..."

"What's today's date again?"

"I've told you. 1st April... Oh God. Somebody hold him still while I hit him."

But she didn't mean it. She went out with her licence and a smile on her face.

The same day, I told another customer that a recent ruling required car owners to produce a Certificate of Interior Excellence as well as the other documents (it says a lot about the irrationality of governments that he believed me.)

I must apologise to the Post Office for these acts of blasphemy against the bureaucratic gods but we were often encouraged to make the post office more user-friendly and one way of doing this was to show that the various transactions we conducted, though important, were not nearly the matters of life and death that some people - including many postmasters - took them for.

Late in the day the boot was on the other foot and we were frequently inundated with people rushing to the post office with

188

dozens of letters including some "specials". One customer in particular used to appear - just as the five o'clock shadow was descending - with twenty or thirty parcels and expect us to deal with them. His company was called "Bones". There was another customer whose parcels looked as if they might *contain* bones. God knows what he was sending through the post. He assured us that the gothic shapes contained nothing more sinister than motor cycle parts; they looked more like the dissected corpse of a dinosaur.

Other customers had unrealistic expectations of our memories. "Two and one" they'd say as they picked up their pension, meaning two telephone stamps and one television stamp - or was it the other way round.

"You should know by now" one old chap said gruffly when I'd given him the wrong combination. I refrained from pointing out that he was one of a few hundred customers I served in the course of the week. He obviously thought he was more special than that. Mind you, even a year after we'd left the shop and ran it when Rob and Sue took a holiday, he was still unforgiving. "Two and one" he said sternly. "Now don't tell me you've forgotten."

CHAPTER SIX

MEN OF LETTERS

The public took a long time to come to terms with the fact that the Royal Mail and Post Office Counters had become two separate things. Some of them still hadn't cottoned on when we left and blamed us when letters went astray. Mind you, after fourteen years, they hadn't grasped that British Telecom was no longer part of the Post Office either and still thought we were responsible for cleaning the telephone box across the road.

People have a love/hate relationship with the Royal Mail, accepting it as a wonderful British institution but never slow to point out its faults. A regular complaint concerns postage rates. "43p to send a letter to New Zealand." they say "Eight and sixpence!" making this quaint conversion to old money as though money has a permanent value which was fixed some time before the First World War. They always refer to pre-inflationary prices, never to pre-inflationary wages. "I bought my first house for £500. Now it'd cost £120,000. How can anybody afford a house these days?" Not easy I agree if you're still earning £5 a week. Anyway, eight and six to send a letter 12,000 miles doesn't seem quite so outrageous when I point out that it costs 26p (five and twopence) to send one to your next door neighbour. "That's true," they say as though I've just pointed out a universal law, and never say anything on the subject again. (No one's ever said that 26p to send a letter next door *is* ridiculous).

But then people generally are illogical about prices, the television licence being a case in point. They object to paying just under 30p a day for 5 radio stations and 2 television programmes yet hand over £8 for 40 fags without batting an eyelid. "Waste of money," they say. "There's never anything worth watching". But the television still stays on all day and their eyes rarely leave the screen.

To get back to postage, inland rates are universal, and if they weren't, people in the far-flung corners of the British Isles would be discriminated against. The market rate for a letter to the Outer Hebrides would be around £10 - either that or there would be only four deliveries a year with a "special" at Christmas. Universal postage rates are one of our last surviving egalitarian traditions - and let's keep the tentacles of the "free market" off them. Even ardent Thatcherites and people utterly opposed to anything resembling state control are remarkably protective of the Royal Mail, which highlights a contradiction at the heart of modern Conservatism. Commodity-dealing youths on five hundred grand a year screeching their BMW's along narrow country lanes to their weekend retreats sit uneasily with John Major's vision of warm beer, the sound of leather on willow, and old ladies cycling serenely to church. The Royal Mail, particularly the rural postman, is far more a part of the latter picture than the former. So even Michael Portillo might say in his old gung-ho style: "Don't mess with the Royal Mail."

But in spite of the successful resistance to privatisation, the Royal Mail has still come under the influence of the cost-cutting brigade. A great deal has been made of the Royal Mail's need to compete in what has become a much more competitive market. Understandable and admirable as far as it goes. But competition seems to involve little more than making the company "leaner". (Why is it that leaner always collocates with fitter, as though if you are lean you are automatically fit?) Well the Royal Mail has become leaner; it has "downsized" to use the fashionable term. And what happens? No relief postmen. On an increasing number of occasions, our regular postman has to undertake two deliveries and his usual customers receive their mail some time in the afternoon by which time many of them are frothing at the mouth and making a few resolutions about not putting their trust in postal deliveries in the future. It is incredible in this age of faxes and email and the mushrooming of courier companies that the local sorting office is forced to implement a policy which for the sake of a few quid means that around 200 people get their mail four hours late. Another time there was no driver for the evening collection and a sack of first class letters plus two specials sat in our post office overnight.

Such dereliction of duty is disappointing particularly when set against the extent to which the public relies on the service and the faith they have in it. Every day about five o'clock, people would pop their heads round the door and ask in the tones of someone inquiring about the result of a chest X-ray whether the last post has gone. When you say for the zillionth time, "No, it never goes before 5.30", they look surprised. "It's just that it's still got "1" on the post box." "The postman's forgotten to change it," I say and they give me a look which indicates that either a) they don't believe me, or b) in less tolerant times, the postman would have been horse-whipped. Then there are the people who come rushing down the road at 5.29, flushed and breathless and hand the postman a single white envelope with the cry "Thank God I've caught you" expressed in the kind of relieved tones that would normally be reserved for catching the last chariot to heaven, or - less plausibly - the morning bus to Cirencester.

I worry about the future of the Royal Mail in this age of email and cyberspace. So far it's managed to ward off the competition from faxes and telexes (although the telegram was one victim of the electronic advance) and there's sufficient Royal Mail loyalists among the older generation to stave off disaster for a few more years if only because of the distrust which older people have in anything new. People in the older age bracket seem to view all new things - particularly anything to do with computers - as part of a general pattern of modernist corruption. Personally, I'm happy to go along with anything that makes life easier or more pleasant.

My first experience of email was when my daughter was on a ship in the Pacific and I needed to get an urgent message to her. I had her email address so I typed the message on a friend's computer, pressed the instruction "Send Message" and watched the computer do its stuff.

"What's it mean, "message sent"?" I asked, feeling a bit like Fred Flinstone.

"It means it's now on the boat waiting for her to collect," he said and I marvelled. How could the Royal Mail compete with this? It was horses and carts against Ferraris.

"Don't trust it," a customer said when I told him about it the following day. He waved a few overseas letters in my face "This is more reliable."

As he went out I reflected on what he had said. More reliable? To stick a stamp on an envelope, see the envelope disappear into an untidy post office - letters were known (very occasionally) to slip down the side of the filing cabinet - be popped into a bag, see the bag whisked off in a small red van to the vagaries of the local sorting office, then on to Gloucester for more sorting, and off to various parts of the world where less reliable systems would take over its welfare. (In Khartoum we used to by-pass the Sudanese postal system altogether by putting British stamps on our letters and asking someone to post them at Heathrow.). Email takes a second; snail mail (as I believe cyberspace aficionados call it) can take months. The Royal Mail is closer to a message in a bottle than it is to email.

But people still retain a touching faith in the international mail service and are astonished when it lets them down. "That letter I posted to the Central African Republic took three weeks to arrive," they say, as though this is a) surprising, b) worthy of diplomatic intervention and c) I am in some way responsible. My God, sir, thinking of what that letter had to go through to get from here to there it's a miracle it ever arrived at all. Of course, I don't say this. Just mutter a few vaguely sympathetic sounds as I would if I'd been told a middle range relative had died.

Part of the respect the average citizen (particularly in rural areas) has for the Royal Mail is down to their affection for the postman. At his best, the rural postman, like the village post office, is an embodiment of all that's good in small communities. He is a fund of gossip and information (Willy Nilly's cry in *Under Milkwood* that "Myfanwy still loves you" as he delivers her love letter is not that much of an exaggeration). Rural postmen visit old ladies, provide ongoing checks on their health and safety and occasionally deliver items from the village shop. The best of the rural postmen do this, and one of the best of the rural postmen in our area is Roger Jackson who has a range of knowledge and intelligence way above the average. (All this means of course is that he shares our attitudes and has the same sense of humour). He enjoys a joke, and can talk football and cricket with a modicum of sense.

Roger burst into our lives one afternoon as I was completing the end-of-day documents with the cry "Beware Ahab, the White Whale is upon thee." For the first time in thirty years, I was projected back into my American literature course not by any of the academics I had encountered in the interim, but by the local postie. I was so surprised, I messed up the the documentation and got an error notice (that's my excuse). "Nearly time for a Jacobite rebellion," he exclaimed a few days later and in response to my bemused look, pointed to the clock. "Seventeen twenty five."

Roger is also by far the tardiest of our postmen, his role as a sort of conversational toy boy for elderly ladies assuming at least equal importance with his official duty of delivering letters. Mind you, it isn't only old ladies he talks to. The post is pronouncedly later if Swindon Town have won (unlikely) or if England is doing well in a test match (unheard of until recently). When a different postman is on duty, the mail is much earlier. Our attitude was always "Yes, you may well have your mail in time for breakfast but can you guarantee that Mr. Jones has had a chance to discuss the budget, or that Miss Murphy hasn't fallen down and broken her leg?" On one of our hired videos, we caught a preview of the film *The Postman* which contained the line "You ain't no postman. You's just a drifter who found a bag of mail." That line must have been written with Roger in mind. Later in the film, one of the baddies sticks a gun up the postman's nose and asks "How much mail can a *dead* postman deliver?" "A damn sight more than our live one," might be the response from the less tolerant residents.

At some stage, Roger was phased out of the evening collection and became a morning specialist (or early afternoon as the cynics would have it). One of his replacements was a bubbly woman called June. June was fifty-five going on twenty and her cheery greeting immediately livened up the place. We developed a song and dance routine to accompany her collection. June was a bundle of inefficient energy, leaving her keys in the post box with the door open on one occasion, forgetting to close the van doors so that mail bags were decanted all along the road on another (now that could never happen to email.) Yet she never seemed to get into trouble or be unduly concerned.

June worked the afternoon shift on Monday, Tuesday and Wednesday. Thursdays and Fridays were covered by somebody else and initially, the end-of-week men measured up to June in their good nature and ability to share a joke. Then a chap took over who we unaccountably christened "Legs". Legs was almost unique in our experience of postmen in that he had the sense of humour of the Ayatollah. One day he came into the shop spitting blood.

"If there's one thing I can't STAND it's GT owners who drive at forty five miles an hour. There's nothing worse."

"Been to Bosnia lately?" I asked but it went over his head.

"Happy New Year " I said one New Year's Eve only to receive the response "*Don't* bloody well wish me a Happy New Year. don't like it."

In some moods, Legs was a pleasant enough fellow, in others he complained about everything; too much mail, too little mail; too much work, too little work; the way people parked, the way they drove. I used to call him "my boy" and he took offence at that. changed it to "my man" and he took offence at that. I came to the conclusion that there was nothing I could say to him that he wouldn't take offence at so I gave up talking altogether. And he took offence at that!

On one occasion, I was serving Rhydian Hughes, a twelve-year-old Welsh lad who, like his elder brother, is a football fanatic. Or rather he is an Arsenal fanatic which may or may not be the same thing. It's a passion they've inherited from their dad which makes one wonder about the irresponsibility of some parents and gives new point to the old saying about the sins of the fathers. On the grounds that all Arsenal supporters are hooligans, I frequently threatened to ban Rhydian from the shop and I certainly made life difficult for him if he came in wearing his Arsenal shirt.

On the day in question, I had been teasing Rhydian about his Arsenal allegiance when one of our pensioners admitted very sheepishly that he too was an Arsenal fan. At this moment Legs entered. "Look out," I cried pointing to the twelve-year-old Rhydian and the small, wiry pensioner. "They're Arsenal supporters. They'll break your leg as soon as look at you!"

Legs began breathing heavily. "If they try anything with me, I'll knock their teeth down their throats!"

You see what I mean about the Ayatollah.

Rhydian Hughes did have a sense of humour and took all my jibes about his football team with the pinch of salt I intended. One evening his mother sent him to the shop to buy some leeks. In good weather (which we sometimes have) our vegetables were kept outside and as I had several other customers, I told him to help himself. He was gone so long I'd forgotten about him and when he did come back he was holding a celery heart. I sent him to look again and this time he came back with a cauliflower! This was particularly amusing as Rhydian, as you've probably gathered, is Welsh. "A true patriot, our Rhydian," his mother said when we told her.

But back to the postmen, or more particularly to Legs. One afternoon I was having a quiet moan about something or other when Legs came in. "You think *you've* got problems," he said in his nasal drawl. "All the men in the sorting office want to have sex with me."

If in the course of my sojourn on this ball of clay I have heard a more amazing statement I certainly don't remember. I looked at Legs and tried to collocate him with the concept "having sex". I tried to picture the local sorting office as a sort of bureaucratic Cromwell Street where a dozen uniformed Fred Wests inflicted untold abuse on innocent newcomers and I couldn't. Either the process of sorting a couple of sacks of first class letters caused workers to lose all self-control or Legs was telling porkies.

"Well we all have our crosses to bear," I said when I had recovered my power of speech.

"It's all right for you," he said grumpily. "You're not the one they want to have sex with." Briefly wondering if the question had ever been discussed, I ushered him out and locked up for the night, suddenly thankful for small mercies.

PART SIX

LAST ORDERS

CHAPTER ONE.

BAPTISM OF FIRE

We have now retired and in the unlikely event of our having the merest inkling of regret, all we need to do is peek out in the morning just before Rob opens the shop and see the early morning customers hovering outside. Our buyers, Rob and Sue, have unfortunate names for the owners of a business. We trust the customers will see them as nominative rather than instructive. As Lizzie remarked a few weeks before they took over: "Let's hope in a few months time it's not Sob and Rue."

Their first morning in charge wasn't promising. At half past eight, Rob popped his head into our cottage with a cry of "Help. I can't cope." Halfway through my first piece of retirement toast though I was, I leapt to his aid. And fully understood his consternation.

Outside the shop were the fishman, who isn't at all intrusive, the dry cleaning man, who is, the man delivering the steel cabinet Rob had ordered to protect his stock from mice, the bread delivery man, plus a couple of lost souls looking for directions. And to top it all, the Post Office trainer. In the face of all this, Rob's cry of "I can't cope," qualifies as one of the great understatements. I tried to reassure him with the glib "It 'll get better" but his blank look indicated that he didn't believe me or he hadn't heard. Either was understandable. The situation wasn't helped by the handle on the front door of the house coming off in Sue's hand, making it impossible to get in or out.

As I said, hardly a typical morning. And neither was their first day typical. A cash and carry trip in the evening became something of a nightmare. I went with them but even Sue failed to respond to my attempts to inject some humour into a pretty sombre occasion. We didn't hear the fifteen-minute warning that the store was closing and were by far the last people there. Two cars stuck in the middle of a dark and rainswept car park were the image of desolation and Sue stood there, helpless, longing for the security of her old life in her country cottage, her tears soaking into the lapel of my jacket. I hadn't the heart to repeat "It'll get better". I just helped them get home as quickly as possible.

It could only have got better. And it did.

But not for a while. Their baptism wasn't helped by having a Post Office trainer for whom the phrase lateral thinking didn' exist. His name was Duncan and I'm sure it's only a matter of time before he meets his Macbeth. Had Sue been her usual acerbic self she would probably have quoted Lady Macbeth:

"The raven himself is hoarse that croaks the fatal entrance o Duncan under my battlements." At the time, Sue hadn't quite worked out where her battlements were, or whether Rob's "vaul ing ambition" hadn't "o'erleapt itself" when he decided to becom a shopkeeper.

Duncan was a bureaucrat, pure and simple who didn't seem t understand that different post offices are different kinds of orgar isms. Crown offices, suburban sub offices, village post offic stores, while fulfilling similar functions are all different animal and a degree of flexibility is needed when dealing with thes different types. Duncan was a nice, pleasant, gentle man with th flexibility of a crowbar.

It wouldn't matter so much if training didn't take place on th job, which means that customers who are as familiar as air to th outgoing staff suddenly find themselves (in what they rightl think of as *their* post office) being treated like strangers and sub jected to all kinds of restrictions which they find at best irksom and at worst offensive.

During an afternoon when he had little to do, Duncan reorganised all the post office drawers so that later, when Rob asked us where to find a particular form, we had no idea. So perhaps Post Office Counters should issue an instruction to their trainers. "Make sure that any changes you make will actually *improve* the situation for the incoming postmaster, otherwise do nothing."

Rob's settling in period as a whole was like a full-scale obstacle course and we could only admire his fortitude as he cleared the hurdles one by one. While we hear frequent platitudes from politicians and the like about the importance of village shops, one wonders whether these observations have penetrated the fortress of local government. Local officials responded sympathetically to the case for Business Rate relief for village shops, while in a department just along the corridor another scheme is being hatched to extort money from them. What the right hand giveth, the left hand taketh away.

One example of such extortion was the transfer of the drinks' licence. When *we* came into the business, the transfer was achieved in one brief court appearance. The magistrate accepted that if we were upstanding enough for the Post Office to trust us with thousands of pounds worth of stock and cash, we could be trusted to administer the few aspects of the licensing laws that applied to us. Not anymore. Before the licence could be transferred, Rob had to attend a two-day course dealing with all aspects of the drinks trade. Then he had to take an exam on the eve of which he was swotting like an undergraduate before finals. When he passed he was given a certificate which he then presented to the court as evidence that he was worthy of a licence. The whole process cost around a hundred and fifty pounds (excluding staff wages) and all for the right to sell maybe twenty five bottles a week. The situation was made more absurd by the fact that he had been selling liquor for several months even though he was neither authorised nor "qualified" to do so. Surely a check list of important points - ensuring customers buying alcohol are over eighteen, not storing alcoholic drinks where they could be stolen by the general public etc - with the threat of visits from a "mystery shopper" to ensure that the laws are being observed is all that should be necessary. Once again, the authorities have failed to distinguish between different kinds of institutions, treating a village shop as if it was a pub or hotel. "Sledgehammer", "crack" and "nut" are the respectible words that come to mind. "Easy" and "money" are others.

Then there was the menace of the Environmental Health Officers. Rob's first visit from an EHO left him seriously concerned about closure. Although we had complied with all the authority's demands down the years, Rob's inspector implied that we had done nothing and he was presented with a list of "essential" work all involving crippling building costs. We were forced to ask why this work hadn't been required of us. The answer is twofold. Firstly, Environmental Health Departments, like other regulatory bodies, have a habit of moving the goal posts so that what was within the rules a year ago is now unacceptable. Secondly, Rob's inspector was newly-qualified and wanted to make an impression. On his second visit, he was substantially more amenable and we like to think that someone in the department had had a quiet word with him. This still begs the question as to why a newly-qualified officer with little on-the-job experience should be assigned to such a sensitive and vulnerable establishment as a village shop in the first place, particularly one that was under new ownership.

I mention all this to provide a contrast with *our* settling in period and to show that, whatever the politicians may claim, things really are getting substantially more difficult for small shopkeepers.

Meanwhile, as the licencing and environmental health regulations are cutting increasingly into the shopkeeper's profits, so their benign cousins on the Rural Development Commission are singing the praises of village shops and offering loans and grants and other assistance. The whole thing reveals a typical lack of co-ordination another case of the right hand not knowing what the left hand is doing. When I hear of experiences like Rob's first EHO inspection or the saga of the drinks' licence, I feel a surge of anger followed by an overwhelming sense of relief that we're out of it, that doesn't directly concern us anymore. We may not see ourselves as Prince Hal, but we have certainly come into our kingdom, out of reach of bureaucrats and bankers. To again quote Shakespeare, we have achieved our taste of heaven

.... by breaking through the foul and ugly mist
Of vapours that did seem to strangle (us).

CHAPTER TWO

ALL'S WELL THAT ENDS WELL

I once said to Lizzie that, like Bing Crosby who died after hitting a perfect drive on the golf course, I would probably drop dead on the day I achieved the perfect post office balance. The seven pence deficit I managed in September 1989 was a close call. I never came closer as my teaching commitments on Wednesday nights meant that Lizzie took on the weekly torture. And yet we felt that, in spite of accounts never quite balancing, and the genuine complaints we had about officialdom and local apathy, our decision to buy a post office enabled us to achieve a balanced lifestyle.

But in the life we chose there were many balances that had to be struck; between the shop and the post office; between the home which occupied most of the building, and the business which occupied the rest; between making money and giving public service; between the humour and lightheartedness essential to the well-being of a village shop and the seriousness of ensuring its survival; between the people that used us because they believed in the shop's survival and those that did so because they needed to; between the people we saw as customers and the customers we came to value as friends. There were compromises too; the compromise between a working arrangement which enabled us to have regular daily breaks from the business but made it difficult to organise longer breaks together; the compromise between the income had both of us taken outside jobs and the absence of travelling time, the avoidance of traffic jams, petrol bills, and the wear and tear on vehicles and nerves, just a few of the stresses that a full-time job in the modern rat race might have brought.

In spite of the occasional cynicism and doubts, we never regretted our decision. Running a village stores enabled us to see people from all classes, many different lifestyles and we were never under any illusions about the poorer members of our community, never felt - as so many better-off people do - that deprivation is a matter of choice rather than need. We served the rich, the well off and the comparatively poor. A village stores, like the village it represents, is "a world in a grain of sand" (to borrow the title of the official history of Poulton). And village shopkeepers get a view of this world in all its aspects.

So we passed on the management of Poulton Village Stores. An
having left, it sometimes seems we were never there - even thoug
we live next door and use the shop daily. It seems impossible tha
for so many years we ran the place, opened it, stocked it, closed i
praised it and cursed it by turns, and it comes as a shock to fin
that things you thought were woven into the very fabric of you
being can disappear from your consciousness as though they'
never existed. I suppose it proves that nothing is forever and n
one is indispensable. One of our older residents recently gave me
verse which I think is worth quoting.

> *Some day when you're feeling important*
> *Some day when your ego's in bloom*
> *Some day when you have that old feeling*
> *You're the number one man in the room,*
> *Take a bucket and fill it with water*
> *Stick your hand in it up to the wrist*
> *Pull it out and the hole that remains there*
> *Is the measure of how you'll be missed.*
> *You may splash all you wish when you enter*
> *Stir the water then stir it some more*
> *But you'll find when you finally leave it*
> *It's exactly the same as before.*
> *As you follow your daily agenda*
> *Always doing the best as you can*
> *Yes, be proud of yourself, but remember*
> *There is no indispensable man.*

While we ran the post office we were sometimes under th
illusion that *we* were indispensable. Well, we weren't and Rob an
Sue are now successfully installed. They emerged from their ear
skirmishes still convinced that they had made the right decisio
And we are also successfully installed - in our cottage next doo
Several people have remarked, "You're looking well; retireme
suits you." Our response is always: "Retirement suits us no matt
how we're looking."

Leaving the shop has also underlined to us its value and th
shortsightedness of villagers who don't respond to the periodic ple
to "use it or lose it." To date, we haven't lost it and for ourselv
we wouldn't be without it. We can now say with no suspicion
having an axe to grind how convenient it is that Poulton still has
shop. We are always popping in - for milk and a newspaper in t
morning and for the odd item in the course of the day.

Of course we do most of our shopping at the supermark
Those places that a few months ago we so deplored have becor

204

essential to making the most of our retirement income. But the shop is essential too. We aim to spend about £20 a week there - twice the amount we implored all Poulton households to spend to keep it viable. It brings home to us how small an effort would be needed to guarantee the survival of all village shops if villagers would only pull together. We've explained in the course of this book how shops can be saved and indicated in our customer profiles and the social problems we had to deal with some of the the reasons they are worth saving, not only or even primarily as retail institutions but more as communal establishments, focal points, places which turn communities. A shop is the heart of the village. Perhaps more than any other establishment, it is the place that gives a village its identity.

Hopefully, some of the people who don't use their shop will read this book and ponder; not just in Poulton but in all the other villages that still have a shop. We watch Rob and Sue making their efforts - croissants at the weekend, wine of the month, new flavours, new lines, new arrangements and now even a total refurbishment - all laudable, all what any enterprising business couple would do. Their efforts villages into deserve appreciation and response. Sadly, as in our early initiatives, the response will probably come from customers already committed. Village shop marketing tends to be about adjustments at the margins.

As I've remarked ad nauseam, Poulton, unlike many villages, still has a shop and we all need to work to keep it. Not only because it's convenient - which it is; not only because it keeps property prices buoyant - which it does; not only because it provides a lifeline for many of our older residents - which it emphatically does. All these things are important but above all we need to keep it for what it contributes to Poulton as a whole. There cannot be a single resident who doesn't feel that, if the shop closed, the village would have lost something not easily replaced.

We still take over the shop from time to time when Rob and Sue want a holiday or a weekend break. These are pleasant times, chances to become re-acquainted with old routines and old customers, to have a taste of what life used to be like. It also reminds us how lucky we are to have retired while young enough to enjoy it. It's a bit like having grandchildren - all the fun and little of the responsibility, knowing that however tiresome they become, however badly they behave, on Monday they will be handed back to their parents.

There are many aspects we miss on a practical basis. We miss having a constant supply of food, wine and ready cash - before we left the post office, we'd never once used a cash point machine. Adjusting to life as customers of banks and shops and off licences was difficult - but we've managed it. We also miss the customers, the chat, the gossip, our position at the centre of village life rather than being consigned to the periphery.

But then there were the bread orders, the vegetable orders, post office stock, post office balances, fridge temperatures in summer, mice in winter, auditors and Environmental Health Officers, the endless round of ordering, selling, paying, calculating, the omnipresent feeling that, in spite of the quiet and frequently enjoyable nature of the work, our lives were never truly our own. This morning (a Sunday) I went into the shop to hear Marlene on the phone to W.H.Smith (in the history of business, can there ever have been a more inefficient organisation?) The supplies of three or four newspapers hadn't arrived. I made sympathetic noises but found it hard to control the smugness as I realised it was no longer my problem. I was about to add that the responsibility of ensuring the shop's survival is no longer our problem either but this isn't strictly true. Of course Rob and Sue have a responsibility to manage the shop in the interests of the village but the responsibility for its survival is a shared one. As Poulton residents we still share that responsibility.

In the course of this narrative, I have frequently mentioned our predecessors, Harold and Jessie, and our successors, Rob and Sue. If I have sounded in any way patronising - impatient towards the former, condescending towards the latter - I apologise. It's really only the way we treat our parents and the way we treat our children. As George Orwell remarked: "Each generation imagines itself to be more intelligent than the one that went before and wiser than the one that came after."

POSTSCRIPT.

As a final note you might like to consider the following comments about life as a village shopkeeper:

Oh how dull is trade and how very scarce is money. Never did I know so bad a time before. I sell my goods as cheap as ever I did...and use my customers with as good manners as ever I did. But trade in all places, and more particularly in a country place, is very precarious ... and what I shall do for an honest livelihood I cannot think.

Familiar complaints, yes, but isn't the language rather quaint? Well it should be. It was written by Thomas Turner in his *Diary of Village Shopkeeper* in 1760. Concern for the future of village shops not, after all, a uniquely contemporary phenomenon.

BIBLIOGRAPHY.

Thomas Turner — *The Diary of a Village Shopkeeper.*

Tom Boyd — *A World in a Grain of Sand.*

Gloucestershire Women's Institutes — *The Gloucestershire Village Book*